How to Teach Yourself and Your Family to Swim Well

by Charles Sava

with Charles D. Champlin

Illustrations by Robert Riger

SIMON AND SCHUSTER / NEW YORK / 1960

Contents

Foreword

By Ann Curtis Cuneo, Former U.S. Olympic Swimming Champion

Charlie Sava, the man who wrote this book and who was my coach for so many fondly remembered years, was once described as "a fiercely capable man with a mind as flexible as a steel girder." It has always struck me as the perfect description of him, because Charlie is completely and passionately devoted to one subject—good swimming.

He has been teaching good swimming for thirty years, mostly for the city of San Francisco, and as nearly as he can figure, he has taught seventy-five thousand people to swim—so far. He has taught Red Cross instructors and lifeguards, thousands of servicemen, adults, teen-agers and, most important, children. He has written about swimming in magazines and newspapers, talked it on television and, primarily, at the Crystal Plunge, the stately and historic pool that was his scene of operations for years. The Plunge finally wore out; Charlie is going stronger than ever. These days his forum is San Francisco's splashy new Larsen Pool.

He has been enormously successful, not only as a teacher of those who swim for fun but also as a coach of competitive swimmers. His Crystal Plunge teams won eight straight national AAU Women's Swimming Championships and many of his pupils have set national and world records.

With all his pupils, but especially with his team swimmers, Charlie is a perfectionist, and his insistence on perfection makes him at times a wonderful blend of devoted father and tough drill sergeant.

As an instance of the drill sergeant in operation, I think often of a meet at the Fleishhacker Pool in San Francisco, after I had been one of Charlie's pupils for three years. I was competing in the 880-yard free style and at the end of that distance sprinted on to see what I could do at the 1,000 meter distance. Because I was in the water, I didn't hear the public-address system announce that I had broken the world's records in both the 880-yard and 800-meter events. I climbed out of the pool and asked Charlie what my time had been. "Never mind your time," Charlie snapped. "That turn you made in the fifth lap was the lousiest I've ever seen in my life." And so saying he stalked away.

That sounds pretty harsh, but Charlie's rigorous attention to details has produced fabulous feats by many of his top swimmers. For example, Marilyn Sahner had long been considered a fine sprint swimmer. But everyone in the swim world except Charlie, who had entered her in the event, was stunned when she broke the national record in the 1,500-meter free style.

Charlie's zeal has not lessened over the years. Not long ago, one of his team swimmers was a girl who trained every afternoon from the time school let out until exactly six-thirty, when she had to hurry home for supper. One afternoon the girl swam a mile, kicked a mile and sprinted ten laps. With that, she climbed out of the pool and headed for the dressing room. "Leaving?" cried Charlie. "It's only six-twenty-seven. You've got time for five more laps."

Such total dedication has brought honors to Charlie as well as to his swimmers. He has received the Helms Award (for his contribution to swimming), the Elliott Award of the AAU's Pacific Association, service-organization awards almost without number and, in 1948, was named Coach of the Year.

Many swimming techniques now accepted as standard were considered radical—or were unheard of—when Charlie first began teaching them. The Red Cross and most swim coaches now teach Charlie's methods on the straight-arm recovery in the crawl, synchronization of breath-ing and arm motion, and other techniques which he sets forth in this book.

As a teacher, Charlie has an almost uncanny ability to instill confidence in his pupils. I sometimes think he is able to hypnotize them. Whatever their fears, their feelings of physical inadequacy, their previous failures in the water, they respond to Charlie's infinitely patient, calm guidance, and in spite of themselves they soon find they are swimming—and swimming well. And to me, the most pleasing and rewarding thing about this book is that Charlie's quiet, reassuring competence comes through in print, too.

Words from the Coach

In his fourth decade of teaching swimming, Charlie Sava was sketched at San Francisco's fine new Larsen Pool, which he runs and where he turns out thousands of able swimmers.

YOU CAN LEARN TO SWIM. Anyone can. Over the last three decades, I've taught preschool toddlers and an eighty-year-old dowager who wanted to learn in a hurry because she had been invited to a week-end pool party. I've taught the deaf and the blind and the lame. I've taught children, thousands of them, and parents who wanted to keep up with their children and enjoy the pleasures of family swimming. I've taught adults who had been tossed into the water as children to "learn," been scared half to death and avoided the water ever after, positive they could never be taught to swim. I've watched swimming turn scrawny kids into strong and vigorous young men and women, bring new fitness to men and women in their middle years and, most of all, bring a new world of enjoyment to everyone who tries it.

Swimming is fun—more fun than any other sport I know. Climbing from a pool or striding to shore after a brisk swim is one of life's most pleasurable moments. It's well-nigh perfect exercise, whose therapeutic values have long been recognized. (President Roosevelt's remarkable resurgence from his crippling bout with polio was due in large measure to swimming.) But swimming's happiest advantage, it seems to me, is that it's the ideal family sport. Because it has virtually no age limits, Grandpa can swim along with his young grandchildren. Everyone can join in the fun and no one has to sit on the sidelines.

This book is aimed at the family. It is, first and foremost, for parents who want to teach their children how to swim. But it is just as applicable to grownups who have never learned to swim and who want to learn. It is, finally, a book for those of any age who have never learned to swim well —to whom swimming is hard work and not much fun. Those who cannot swim at all can learn how in this book. Those who swim a little can learn how to swim better, more easily, safely, pleasurably.

In my thirty years of teaching seventy-five thousand people how to swim, I've developed and proved a foolproof, step-by-step method. That method, as set forth in this book, takes up the component parts of swimming one by one. As the pupil masters each part, he's also getting used to the water, becoming familiar with it, at ease in it. At last the parts go together and he's swimming.

In the pool, I have most pupils swimming in two weeks. Sometimes it takes a little longer, sometimes less. Individuals differ, particular in the fear of water they may have acquired over the years. But in most cases, *if you adhere carefully to the sequence of lessons presented here,* you should be able to teach someone else to swim in about two weeks—or to learn to swim yourself in that time.

Very young children present special problems, requiring endless patience and the right approach. That's why this book begins with a special section devoted to the very young. Many parents have tried to teach their children to swim and given up in frustration. It's easy—if you know how. And this book will tell you how, from the moment the child first splashes into the water until he's doing the dog paddle.

For everybody except the very young, the teaching technique does not change. It remains the same for the six-and-up group to any eager octogenarians in the audience. As I said above, this technique involves taking the various parts of swimming, mastering them one by one and finally combining them like the parts of a model plane. Once the youngsters have got to the dog paddle stage, they should go back and start again with the lessons in Part Two, Family Swimming. Occasionally there are special tips and hints that are helpful in the teaching of younger pupils. These I've added at the end of the chapters in Family Swimming—in blue type, like this.

This book thus begins with the simplest possible language and the most rudimentary water activities. But it goes on to include championship techniques in the American crawl and to introduce you to one of the greatest thrills the sport has to offer, swimming in the surf. I've tried to make this the most complete and most useful book about swimming ever written. Using the method presented here, anyone can learn, or be taught, to swim. And anyone who can swim a little can learn to swim better.

There are too many people everywhere who don't know how to swim. Millions more don't really know how to swim well. Everyone should know. Every drowning is a needless tragedy, and for that reason alone people should learn how to stay alive. But the safety aspect of knowing how to swim is not primarily what I've had in mind in writing this book. Everyone should learn because it is the open-sesame to uncountable, unbeatable hours of pleasure for the individual and for the whole family. I hope that this book, with my words and Bob Riger's clear and vivid illustrations, will be the open-sesame you've been waiting for.

I should like at this point to acknowledge a genuine debt of gratitude to my former student, Marilyn Sahner, whose encouragement and helpfulness in the preparation of this manuscript have been invaluable.

And now, happy swimming!

CHARLES SAVA

10

Don't Go Near the Water—Yet

Now, THEN, before we get into the pool or the lake to see if the water is warm enough, let's take up two fundamentals. They ought to be repeated in every chapter, they're so important. And they're important whether you're a parent about to lead your children to the water's edge, or an instructor about to help someone else's children, or a self-starter bravely going it alone.

Make Friends with the Water.

Air, not water, is man's natural element. Often our first reaction to water is to be afraid of it, and it's a natural reaction. At some time or another all of us have caught a noseful of water and found it unpleasant. The youngest child, if he's ever had an hour at lake- or seaside, has probably been buffeted by a wave or has stumbled over a wave and inhaled some water. As a result, he's cautious if not downright timid. And rightly so. And right here let's demolish the old myth that the best way to get a child to swim is to throw him into the water. This sink-or-swim method has done a thousand times more harm than good, and even the youngsters who have somehow swum have developed a terror of the water that takes years to overcome. From the very beginning, swimmers should develop a healthy respect for the water and also learn to be at home in it. The child, or any nonswimmer, who feels afraid of the water will be a long time learning to swim. From the beginning the learner should work at feeling at home in the water. Sit in it, splash in it. At each step in the lessons the learner should feel relaxed and confident, at ease and in charge, before moving on to the next step.

The youngsters will have trouble understanding this, but everybody should keep in mind what the teachers say: "Any object immersed in a solution tends to be buoyed up by a force equal to the weight of the liquid displaced." In other words, if when you're in swimming your body occupies a space equal to fifty pounds of water, you're supported by a force equal to fifty pounds. Water has supporting power; you can float, like a piece of wood or an inner tube. Folks who swim great distances—across the English Channel, let's say—have learned this lesson well. Floating on their backs, they can rest almost as completely as if they were lying in bed. Floating is an essential of good swimming. It's more than that; by itself, it can save your life. The youngsters can see that a piece of wood, without arms or legs, floats. This simple knowledge should help them, or you, or anyone, overcome an uneasiness about being in the water. The water will help you to swim—if you let it.

Take It Slowly.

This is the second, vital fundamental of learning to swim. Whether you and your pupils are in the very early stages of learning to float or have begun learning to paddle, keep all your movements slow and deliberate. Sudden and erratic movements are the bane of good swimming—and the quickest way to invite a noseful or mouthful of water. Pretend that you're seeing yourselves in slow motion. Plan your moves and keep them slow and under control. You'll save yourselves many an unwanted swallow of water and make it that much easier to acquire that all-important feeling of being confident and at ease in the water.

Water can be your servant. Make yourself its master.

Part One

TEACHING THE VERY YOUNG TO SWIM

WITH A LITTLE parental patience, very young children can be taught to be reasonably polite to Aunt Harriet when she comes calling or to handle a spoon tolerably well. Teaching them to swim is something else again—a chore that has shattered the patience of parents without number.

The one great problem in teaching a child (or anyone else, for that matter) to swim is getting him used to having his face in the water. Most youngsters, even at three, have learned that a noseful of water, in bathtub or lake, can be unpleasant. Occasionally a news picture comes along showing a tot who, though barely able to walk, can swim like Gertrude Ederle. In most cases, these precocious paddlers have learned to swim before they learned to be fearful—or respectful—of the water. Overcoming these fears requires endless patience and gentleness, plus a careful plan of attack that most parents lack.

Very young children present special problems. They can't concentrate very long. They're not yet well co-ordinated. They can't understand the principles involved—flotation, for example. They can't always understand verbal instructions. They need to be *shown,* and they can't be hurried.

This special section takes these special problems in hand. It's aimed specifically at teaching very young children, age three to perhaps age six. It's simple, brief and nontechnical. In eight easy steps, the youngster learns to overcome his fears of the water and makes his way to the dog paddle and a rudimentary, head-out-of-the-water crawl. When he has mastered these, he (and Mom and Dad or the instructor) can move on to the lessons in the main section of this book.

The best way to start tiny tots on the road to swimming, I've found, is through a series of little games. These games are helpful two ways: They make the water fun, as it should be, and eventually they involve swimming skills.

All of these games are intended for groups, although many can be played by a single child. I've found that it's often more effective to work with more than one child. One child is apt to be more venturesome than another, more willing to try something new. Watching this leader, a timid child may overcome his fears and join in the fun. Pride, the competitive spirit, the simple seeing that "it doesn't hurt," all help the timid child.

Let me note some obvious cautions:

1. The child should be rested and happy and the water shouldn't be too cold.

2. Keep the lessons short. Twenty minutes is about the longest you can hope to keep a child's attention.

3. No matter how sorely tried your patience is, never push a child under the water—to show him, for example, that it doesn't hurt to have his face in the water. You know it, and he'll learn it, but he has to learn it in his own good time.

4. Try to keep the child from getting accidental nosefuls or facefuls. These will only delay the time it takes him to get used to the water. Stay close to the child. Tell him and show him what you and he are going to do.

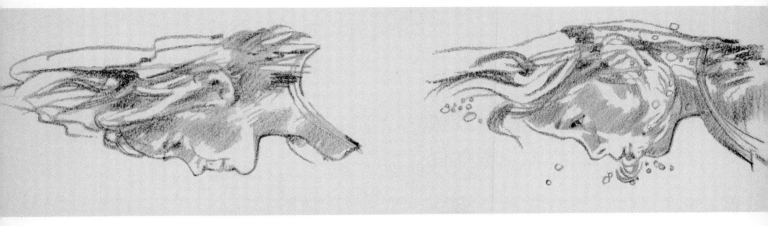

STEP ONE:
The Fun Begins at Home

Right at home in the dead of winter you can get a head start on the big challenge: getting the child used to having his face in the water. Fill the washbasin with water. First have the child hold his nose and duck his face into the water. Make a game of it. As he learns to keep his face in the water, start counting and gradually increase the time until he can hold his face in the water for ten seconds. Be sure he first takes a deep breath through the mouth, then shuts it tightly. Now he has learned not to inhale water through the nose.

Later have him put his face into the water without holding his nose. Be sure he keeps his chin pulled in and his eyes looking down as he submerges. This will prevent water from rushing into his nose. Try having him compress his lips slightly and blow bubbles in the water, imitating the sound of a motorboat. This will be just a game at the moment, but it's the clue to the correct technique for exhaling under water, which is extremely important and which we'll take up in Lesson 2 of the main section of the book. Gradually, too, he can learn to keep his eyes open under water. Try putting pennies in the basin for him to see and retrieve. Don't rush any of this. But a few minutes' play each day— at tooth-brushing time before bed, for example— can have your child ready and eager for the pool or lake when summer comes.

STEP TWO:
Simple Fun in the Water

These first—and simplest—games have three objectives: helping the child overcome his fear of water, showing him how the water will support him, teaching him to keep his balance as he moves through the water.

Train. Join hands, children and adults alternating. One child becomes the "engine," another the "caboose." Then, making train noises—whistles, bells, chug-chugging—the line snakes through the water, sometimes fast, sometimes slow, backing into a siding. Keep to shallow water, knee-deep at most. Take care that the game doesn't get so exuberant that a child falls down and gets a noseful. Besides having a lot of fun, the kids get the feel of the water resistance. They're also getting friendly with the water.

Giant Step. This is simply a water version of the old back-yard game, designed to develop confidence in the water. The children line up in shallow water. Teacher then calls for "one giant step forward," "one giant step backward," tiny step, sideways step, turn-around, and so on.

To give kids an even greater sense of participation in the game, let one of the children call the signals. Just watch carefully that the steps don't lead the other children into deeper water.

Airplane. This game works fine if you're at a pool

or at a lake where there's a dock fairly low in the water.

Have the child sit at the edge of the pool or dock and spread his arms like the wings of an airplane. The teacher, standing in the water, holds him around the chest. At "Go" the child pushes away from the poolside with his feet, belly-flops on the water and, supported by the teacher, glides along the surface like a plane landing.

As the child gains confidence, he can probably be persuaded to leap from the edge into the arms of the teacher, who then supports him for the belly flop and gliding as before.

STEP THREE:
Deeper in the Water

These next, more advanced games aim to get the child used to having his head and entire body under water.

Ring-around-a-Rosy. Form a circle, with an adult for every three or four children. The adult should be holding the youngest or smallest children. Everybody sings the words of "Ring-around-a-Rosy," and at the end "all fall down." Some of the older youngsters will make quite a vigorous game of this. Be sure they don't give the younger kids too much of a ducking. The water should be a little more than knee-deep.

Rain. This makes a game out of being splashed. The children form a circle, then scoop up water and pour it over their heads. Sing "Rain, Rain, Go Away," or any other rain songs they know.

For variation the children can turn their backs to the center and splash water into the circle. Everybody gets splashed on the back.

Faces in the Water. This is the washbasin exercise made into a group activity. The children form a circle in waist-deep water, take big breaths, close mouths, bend over and put their faces flat into the water. Gradually increase the time the youngsters can keep their faces in the water.

Having conquered the business of face under water, try variations: *blowing bubbles,* seeing who can churn up the water the most; *jack-in-the-box,* having the children squat in the water at the teacher's signal, then jump up at the count of three or five.

Opening Eyes under Water. After the children have got used to having their faces in the water, they can learn to open their eyes in the water. Form a tight circle. Put your hand under water in the center of the group. Let the children count how many fingers you're extending. The first one to pop up and give the number is the winner.

A variation: Drop pennies, metal toys or pretty stones in waist-deep water and have the children bend over, find and retrieve them.

STEP FOUR:
A Little Nearer Swimming

Boat. If a child has learned to have his face in the water he's ready for this game, which gets him a little nearer to swimming. It's like the airplane game described above. The child lies flat on the water, supported by the teacher's arms around his chest. Arms are outstretched like the prow of a boat and the child kicks his legs vigorously to churn the water like an outboard motor.

STEP FIVE:
Floating

By now the youngsters should be fairly well used to having their faces in the water. The hardest part of learning to swim is over and the kids are probably rarin' to go. Up to now, they've been able to keep their feet firmly on the bottom or have been supported. This next step—learning to float—for the first time removes that reassuring contact with the bottom. It's a big step, one the youngsters may resist. Mom and Dad, or the teacher, will have to lead them to it slowly, gradually, patiently. Show the tot what he's going to do. Show him it can be done. If Dad is the teacher, let Mom pretend to be the pupil. Remember, children learn by copying; this is as true of swimming as it is of table manners.

16

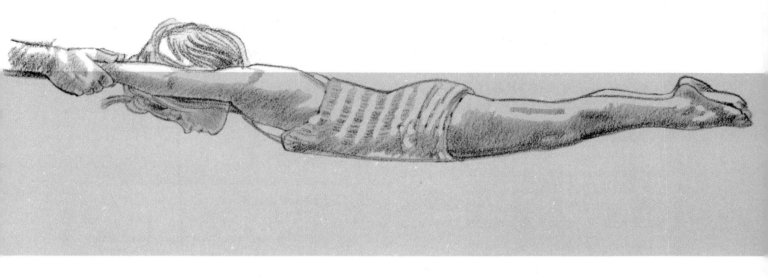

The Jellyfish Float

This float is so easy it's almost a game in itself. Most important, it gives the child instant proof of his ability to float.

Have the child wade into waist-deep water. Have him squat down until his chin touches the water, then clasp his hands just below his knees. He takes a deep breath, holds it and lowers his head into the water. As his feet rise from the bottom, he pulls his knees up against his chest. His chin rests on his chest and his knees and head touch.

He'll be floating like a cork! Only the middle of his back is above the water and he'll roll and bob with the water's motion.

To recover, he has only to release his knees and put his feet to the bottom again. When his footing is firm, he stands up. Make sure he moves slowly, so that he doesn't lose his balance.

Dad should demonstrate the float once, then let the child try it several times.

The Back Float

Stand behind the child in what, for him, is about waist-deep water. Put your hands under his shoulders and have him lean back, keeping his legs and body straight, until he's supported by your hands and his legs rise toward the surface. Still holding him, walk slowly backward and have him kick under water, but not hard. Don't rush through this exercise. It takes a lot of time.

Next, change the position of your hands. Keep one hand under his shoulders, place the other one under his head. The water should come above the ears but the face should be above water. Have him keep his body straight and stretch his arms out so that he becomes a big T. Slowly reduce the support you give his shoulders. It will take several attempts, but eventually he'll be able to float alone.

When he can float alone, teach him to "fin"— to move the hands gently in and out at his sides. Finally, have him kick, a gentle flutter kick. He's moving! Keep close to him all the time, to make sure he doesn't get an accidental ducking.

The Face Float

This is what the kids have always called the "dead man's float." It's also known technically as the prone float.

Stand facing the child in water up to his waist. Take his hands. Have him inhale through the mouth and hold a deep breath. Place his face in the water. Pull him slowly forward by taking two or three steps backward. His legs will rise and

17

he'll float on the surface. Hold him until he has recovered his balance. Repeat this maneuver many times. Then release his hands and let him float free, but stand by to help him regain his balance.

To teach the child to regain a standing position in the water, try this: Have him take a deep breath, hold his nose and sit on the bottom. To stand he will automatically draw up his knees and place his feet flat on the bottom. Have him practice moving to an upright position from the face float, drawing up his knees, then putting his feet flat on the bottom. Just as they should demonstrate the floats, Mom and Dad should do this first, too. Junior will get a big kick out of it.

STEP SIX:
Gliding

Now stand a few feet away from the child. Have him place his arms on top of the water, thumbs linked. He takes a deep breath, puts his face in the water, shoves off with his feet and goes into a glide. Have your arms outstretched, ready to catch him. Gradually increase the distance between you. Eventually he can glide to the dock or pool edge and catch hold himself. (Be sure to stay close to him, however.) If he has a tendency to roll over, his head is probably not low enough in the water.

STEP SEVEN:
Kicking—and How Kids Can
Get a Kick out of It

When the youngster is gliding successfully, let him start kicking. It should be the gentle, relaxed kick that comes naturally to him.

And when he's kicking, he's ready for the delights of a kickboard. A kickboard is a piece of balsam wood about two feet long, eighteen inches wide and one inch thick. Championship swimmers use it to develop their leg muscles. For a tot

Using the kickboard

the kickboard can make learning to swim more fun than ever, and the grownups will get a kick out of it, too.

The first few times the youngster tries the kickboard, the teacher should hold the front end to steady it. The swimmer's arms rests on the board and he grips the sides, toward the front. At first the teacher should stay close by the youngster, because uneven kicking may make him lose his balance. But the child will quickly learn the art of balancing and he'll delightedly find he's propelling himself through the water.

The kickboard is also valuable in teaching a small youngster the face float. Have him hold the board by the back corners. He then takes a deep breath, places his face in the water and pushes himself off the bottom and into a glide. Make it a game to see how far he can glide. Stay close to him until he learns how to regain his footing after the glide. When he's using the kickboard, make sure he doesn't inadvertently kick his way into deep water.

STEP EIGHT:
The Dog Paddle

By the time your youngster is gliding and kicking through the water, you'll be having trouble holding him back. The next thing he needs is the stroke. The dog paddle is the instinctive method by which untutored kids (and animals) learn to swim. It's a good idea to have very young children practice it first, before they try it along with gliding and kicking.

A good way to show the youngster how the stroke works is to have him take hold of the pedals on a tricycle and pump away; he'll quickly see the in-and-out arm motion. Then have the child kneel in water deep enough to cover his shoulders and paddle for a while. When he's got it, have him go into a face float, start kicking and finally paddling. He'll be able to do it for only a few seconds, as long as he can hold his breath— BUT HE'S SWIMMING. Let him try it a few times in

19

the float position, his head still in the water. Then have him swim with his head above the water. He won't be able to swim this way for long distances, either. A child's head is oversized in relation to the rest of his body and his neck muscles will soon tire. But he's swimming and ready for weeks of splashing good fun and pleasure.

Mom and Dad or the teacher should remember, however, that a child, like an adult, can easily overestimate his new-found swimming abilities. Children should never play in the water without responsible supervision.

The next step in swimming is, of course, learning the true crawl, breathing with face in the water. The co-ordination involved here is too tough for the tiny tots whom we've been dealing with in this section. But the majority of my students are ready for it at six, seven and eight. When your tots are paddling expertly enough, turn to Lesson 2, on breathing, and go on from there. Lesson 2 is vitally important to good swimming; don't miss it.

Here, a brief word about floating devices. Inner tubes, air mattresses and life jackets, which give the child total support in the water, may make him feel at ease, but they won't help him learn to swim and may hinder him if he becomes dependent on them. Water wings and small tubes (the kind you find in toy stores) are better because they don't support him totally and they make him kick and paddle. Another good device is the cork belt, the principal advantage of which is that you can remove one cork at a time (unknown to the child) as he becomes more accustomed to the water and as his lessons progress.

Inner tubes and mattresses are dangerous in the hands of the nonswimmer because they can lead him beyond his depth. Life jackets make good sense on boats and in lakes where water depth may vary sharply from place to place. The big point is that a child has to learn to swim without flotation devices eventually and he shouldn't be allowed to depend on them.

Learning the dog paddle, the child first goes into a face float, arms outstretched, as shown below.

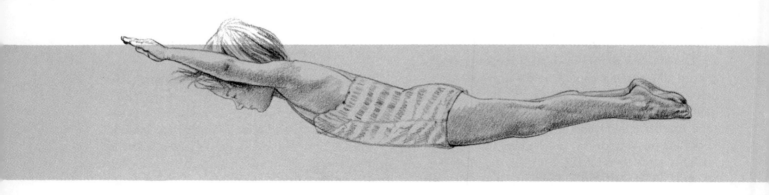

Start kicking, then begin to paddle. You're swimming! When this step is mastered, try it with face out of the water.

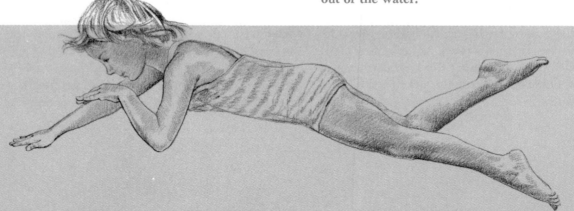

Part Two

FAMILY SWIMMING

Here, in effect, the book begins again. We've dealt with the special problems of teaching small children to swim. Now we're going back to the water's edge to wade in again with everybody else. The fact is that the technique of learning to swim is the same for everyone who is beyond the tot stage. The step-by-step approach is the same one we've used in Part One; but it's now a slightly different set of steps, and the whys and wherefores will be spelled out in a lot more detail.

Throughout the rest of this book, I'm going to be talking directly to the learners themselves, just as I do when I'm teaching my own classes in person. I'll be telling them how to breathe, how to hold their arms, and so on. Of course, the majority of this book's readers will be the mothers and fathers, and not the young learners. Still and all, I think it will keep things a lot clearer and simpler if I tell my imaginary pupil what to do, instead of trying to tell an imaginary teacher what to tell his imaginary student to do. In a sense, this book is a script for parents, providing them with the words to say to their children.

It's worth reminding parents again that the younger the learner is, the more he needs to be shown, as well as told, what he's supposed to do. Parents will do well to try everything first, before they spring it on the kids. Finally, be patient and take it slowly. Master each step as it comes and it's impossible *not* to learn to swim.

Happy learning!

Lesson 1

Getting Your Face Wet

Lᴇᴀʀɴɪɴɢ ᴛᴏ ʙʀᴇᴀᴛʜᴇ is the first step in the process of learning to swim. It's a tough one. In the air, we breathe naturally, without giving it a thought. In the water, breathing has to be a deliberate, calculated action following a regular rhythm. Putting your face under water goes against all human instincts and takes a while to get used to. But you will get used to it, and once you've mastered it you've conquered the toughest, most important part of swimming.

Without getting too technical, here's why breathing is so important: In the first place, proper, rhythmical breathing helps your balance and co-ordination. It makes swimming easier. In the second place, when you swim you need more air. When you exert yourself, your muscles consume more oxygen and you produce more used air (mostly carbon dioxide) which you have to get rid of. Deep breathing gives your body more oxygen and gets rid of the carbon dioxide, increasing your endurance.

Here, finally, we go into the water.

The first job is to get used to having your face in and under the water. To do this, get into shallow water, shallow enough so that you can kneel on hands and knees and have your head and shoulders above the water. (If the shallow end of the pool is over two feet deep, one may stand in the pool with both hands on the edge, facing the

pool wall). Bend your head down so that you're looking straight at the water, as into a mirror. Make sure your chin is tucked in close to your chest. Take a deep breath and hold it. Tighten your lips. Then sʟᴏᴡʟʏ lower your head parallel to the water until it's completely beneath the surface. Keep your eyes open. Count to five. Then sʟᴏᴡʟʏ lift your head from the water and exhale. (If you've kept your head parallel to the water, no water should have gone up your nose.) That wasn't so bad. Now repeat the process. After the first few times, start increasing the count. When you can keep your head under water for ten slow counts, you should be ready to move on.

Remember, make all your movements sʟᴏᴡʟʏ and deliberately. Thrusting the head rapidly into and out of the water will result in water being forced up the nose. By now you should be able to keep your head under water without discomfort or fear.

Now, as a prelude to the next lesson, try this: Tighten your lips slightly and exhale through them—without inflating your cheeks. Don't tighten up enough to blow a bugle, but just enough so that you have to force the air out gently without inflating the cheeks. Some folks may find, doing this, that their lips buzz slightly or vibrate. This is the correct way to exhale with your face in the water. Whether you're swimming

fast and breathing fast or swimming slowly and breathing slowly, you exhale by gently forcing your breath through slightly compressed lips.

There are several important reasons for exhaling through tightened lips. First and foremost, it helps keep water out of your mouth and enables you to breathe through your mouth and nose at the same time. Second, it gives you far better control over the rate at which you exhale. It thus helps you to co-ordinate your breathing with the arm stroke. Finally, it helps you to empty your lungs completely of carbon dioxide, thus reducing fatigue and increasing your endurance.

Try it a few times in chest-deep water. Bend over, face parallel to the surface of the water.

Take a deep breath, slowly put your face under water and exhale through slightly compressed lips.

Even school-age children may boggle at putting their faces fully into the water the first time. If they do, refer back to the games at the beginning of the section Teaching the Very Young to Swim. If it helps, let the child hold his nose and keep his eyes shut the first few attempts. A good underwater performance by Dad—making faces, blowing bubbles, retrieving coins—will help, too. You can't rush the child, and any use of forceful persuasion will only stiffen his resistance and heighten his fears.

The Way Swimmers Breathe

Now, WITHOUT GOING ANYPLACE, we'll take up the technique of breathing that you'll be following when you start swimming. Because it's different from anything you've done before, we'll do a couple of dry runs even before we try it with our faces in the water.

Take the same position as in Lesson 1, kneeling. Turn your head to the right and bend slightly, as if you were laying it on a pillow. INHALE deeply through your mouth. *Immediately* start EXHALING, through both your nose and your slightly compressed lips, and, as you do, rotate your head slowly until it's pointing straight down at the imaginary pillow. In other words, you begin exhaling even before your face turns into the water. Remember that the stress should be on mouth breathing. Still exhaling, turn your head back to its original position. At the moment your head is back to its original position, your lungs should be empty and you should be ready to draw another deep breath and begin a new cycle.

It's unflattering, but for the moment think of your head as an orange, jammed on the end of a sharp stick. The orange can't move up or down, it can only swivel on the end of the stick. In swimming, your head should be the same way. Your spine and neck will stay in a straight line and your head will turn only from right side to straight down—about a quarter of a turn.

When you've tried this kind of breathing a few times just to get the general idea, try it in the water.

Again, take the same position as in Lesson 1, kneeling in shallow water, with your head and shoulders above the water. Turn your head to the right and lay it on the water as you would lay it on a pillow. Your left ear will be under the water, your nose and mouth and eyes out of the water.

INHALE through your mouth. Tighten your lips slightly, as I've described, to keep the water out of your mouth, and SLOWLY turn your head to the left, down into the water. The water should come to your *brow line*. In other words, your head is only shallowly in the water. As you turn, EXHALE through your nose and lips, with stress put on mouth breathing. (Remember that you don't inflate your cheeks.) Then, still exhaling, turn your head back to its original position, lying on the water pillow, nose and mouth just above the water.

If your timing has been right, you're ready to draw another deep breath at the moment your nose and mouth break out of the water.

After this first time, rest a minute. Then repeat the cycle again. Inhale through your mouth. Exhaling, rotate head into the water and back out again. Remember to keep your lips slightly compressed. You should feel them vibrate as you exhale.

There's no question about it, learning to exhale your breath completely while turning your head through the water is tricky. Try one cycle at a time until you have the timing pretty well under control. You should finish breathing out just at the moment your nose and mouth leave the water.

Now run through a few cycles without stopping. INHALE, underwater EXHALE; INHALE, underwater EXHALE; and so on.

Two things may happen: (1) After a few cycles, you're exhausted and gasping for breath.

This almost certainly means that you're not exhaling completely, or it may mean that you're holding your breath for a second or two before exhaling. Your lungs don't get rid of all the spent air and you're not getting enough fresh air and oxygen. To correct the condition, make sure you're exhaling as completely as you can and *immediately*. (2) After a few cycles, you may find yourself getting dizzy. This almost certainly means you're inhaling *too* deeply. Practicing in a kneeling position and not using your arms or legs, you don't need as much oxygen. The need for oxygen is in proportion to your exertion. The harder you work the more oxygen you need. To correct the condition, breathe easier.

This is a tough lesson. You may get a noseful. This way of breathing is not natural, as I noted earlier; it must be learned. Take it slowly, be patient, and you'll master it. Keep at it until you can do one hundred cycles—breathe one hundred times—without stopping, tiring or missing a beat.

Your whole success as a swimmer will depend on how well you learn to breathe. It's worth while to take a lot of time and get it down pat.

At this point, early in the game, I want to stress two things: one, children vary in the facility with which they learn to swim; two, each child should thoroughly master each lesson before he goes on to the next. It's a good idea at the start of each lesson to have the child practice what has gone immediately before. And from time to time it's wise to let the child have a day or two (or more) to practice what he has learned up to that moment, letting the lessons soak in before he goes on.

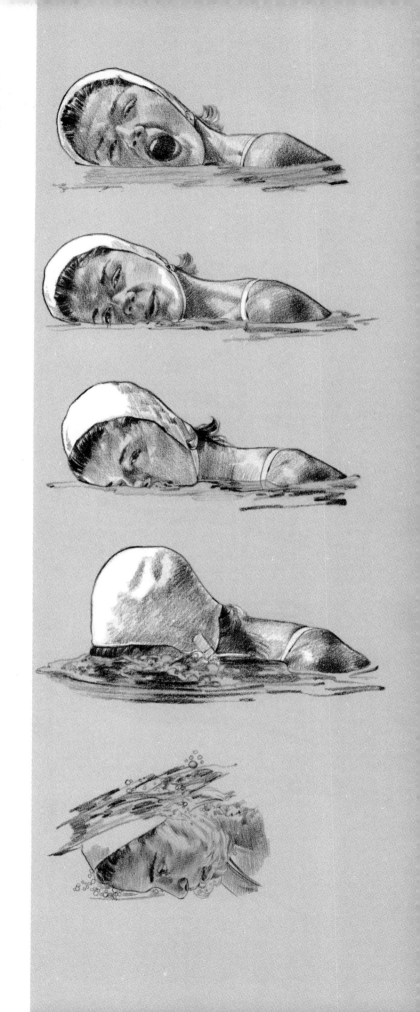

Notice that the swimmer inhales through wide-open mouth and starts to exhale immediately through both nose and compressed lips (to keep water out). The neck position does not change. The head does not lift but swivels as if it were on a stick. The breath should never be held; breathing is continuous.

Kicking without Going Anyplace

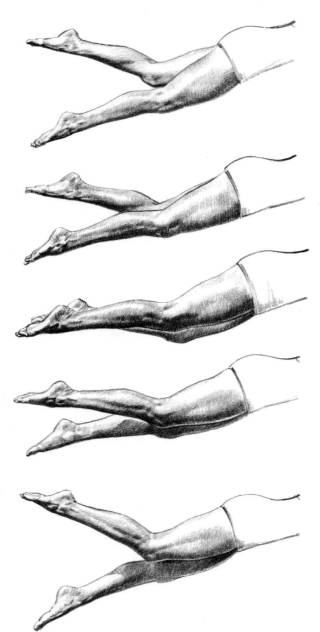

Now you're ready for the second element of swimming: the kick. Kicking is simple, but there's also an art to it, and the right technique will help you get the most power or push from your effort.

To practice the kick, find a place where you can lie chest down in shallow water. Hold on to the pool edge or the dock. If you find your hand grip is not enough to keep your body from sinking, try bracing your forearms against the pool wall or dock, with elbows below your wrists. This time your head stays out of water; we're just kicking.

The leg kick is a whiplike movement that starts at your hips and flows down your relaxed legs to your toes. The kick is also called the *thrash,* and when you've kicked a while you'll see why.

As you kick, your knees bend slightly. Don't try to keep them stiff. Your ankles turn in slightly. (It comes naturally; don't force them.) Your legs should pass as close to each other as possible without actually touching. Your knees should be about an inch apart. There's a reason for this: The farther apart your legs are, the less they churn up the water and the less forward momentum you get. So your legs are held together, relaxed and natural.

Your instep must be arched and your toes pointed. This is extremely important. If your toes aren't extended, no matter how hard you kick you may remain stationary or even move backward. Also, if the toes and instep aren't properly arched and pointed your legs will have more of a tendency to sink.

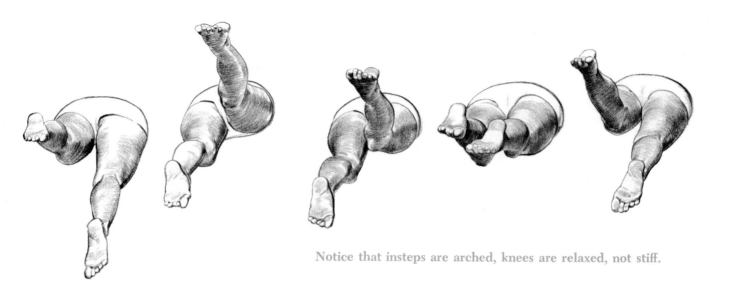

Notice that insteps are arched, knees are relaxed, not stiff.

As your feet kick up and down, they should move about as far from each other as they do when you're walking, about fourteen to twenty inches. In other words, your kick matches your stride. At no time should either foot leave the water completely. Occasionally, kicking hard, the heel and bottom of your foot will break the surface, but that's all. The effort spent breaking the surface and getting the foot back under water takes power away from your forward progress and the kick defeats itself.

The kicking motion is continuous. It thrashes along like a motor, pushing you ahead. The natural rhythm for the kick is one-two-three, one-two-three, like as fast waltz. With a two-beat kick, you'd find yourself favoring one leg over the other: ONE-two, ONE-two—like that. With a three-beat kick, even if you say ONE-two-three, ONE-two-three, the stress keeps shifting from one leg to the other. And actually the kicking is even and steady. Count to yourself as you kick. For now,

to help you perfect the rhythm, count one-two-three, one-two-three. Later on you'll be counting to six, to develop the rhythm for the six-beat crawl. Counting will give you added smoothness, keep your hips from swaying and probably help keep you relaxed.

Remember, it's important that your legs be relaxed, never stiff. If they are relaxed, the knee bend, the depth of the kick and the position of the legs will all work out right.

In your position at the side of the pool or the dock, you should be able to kick for ten minutes —without stopping—before moving on to the next lesson. (It's great exercise.)

Youngsters especially are apt to kick too high and too hard, expending a lot of energy, enjoying the splash but getting very little power. Right now is the best time to see that they kick properly—feet arched, legs together but relaxed, feet staying under the water.

27

Breathing While You Kick

Now you're ready to combine the last two lessons, kicking and breathing. It may strike you as odd to take these up now, even before we've considered the basic business of staying afloat. The reasons are simple: Breathing and kicking are so important to good swimming that I've found it best to introduce them early so that the beginner will have the longest possible time to perfect them. Then, too, the beginner has that much more time to get used to being in the water, before he actually goes on his own.

In Lesson 3 you learned that the rhythm of kicking goes one-two-three, one-two-three. Now, as we co-ordinate kicking with the breathing technique from Lesson 2, we'll make each breath cover six beats or kicks. The co-ordination goes like this:

One: INHALE with head turned to side.
Two: Turn head toward center while EXHALING.
Three: Head straight down at center.
One: Head starts back to side.
Two: Head almost back to starting point.
Three: Head back at side, with nose and mouth out of water, ready to INHALE on *one* and begin a new breathing cycle.

Take the same position in shallow water at the side of the pool, as in Lesson 3, hanging on to the pool or dock, body lying chest down on the water. Start kicking and counting rather slowly. When you've established the rhythm, start the breathing cycle. It will seem at least a little like trying to pat your head and rub your stomach at the same time. Go slowly until it works smoothly.

Keep at it until you can do it for about fifteen minutes, before you go on to the next lesson.

TWO IMPORTANT POINTS FROM THIS LESSON:

1. Always count as you kick. Maintaining the rhythm will keep you from getting lazy. Like a well-tuned motor, your legs will keep you churning along through the water.

2. Don't hold your breath. Your breathing cycle should always be timed so that as your nose and mouth break above the water your lungs are empty and you're ready to draw a deep, full breath. Holding your breath traps the spent air in your lungs and brings on fatigue and exhaustion much faster. If you are holding your breath, it means your timing cycle is wrong and, like a sputtering motor, should be corrected.

For kids particularly, the important thing here is that they get used to kicking steadily and rhythmically and breathing steadily and rhythmically, both at the same time. The timing of one cycle with the other is not yet vitally important; since it may confuse the younger learners, don't worry about it. The kick rhythm is important. To make sure the youngsters get it, Dad should clap out the ONE-two, ONE-two marchlike beat that's WRONG and then the one-two-three, one-two-three waltzlike beat that's RIGHT.

Whether you're using a kickboard (above) or holding the poolside, remember, as you combine kicking and breathing, that you don't lift your head or tilt your body from side to side.

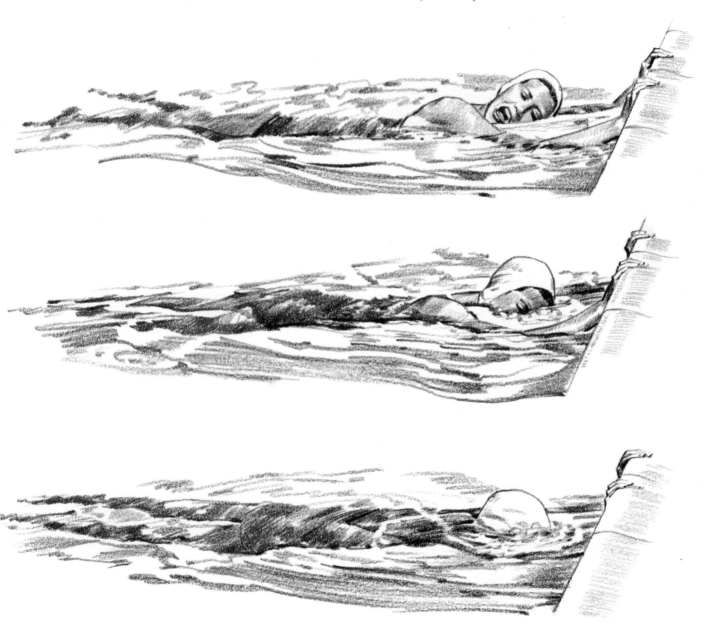

You Too Can Float

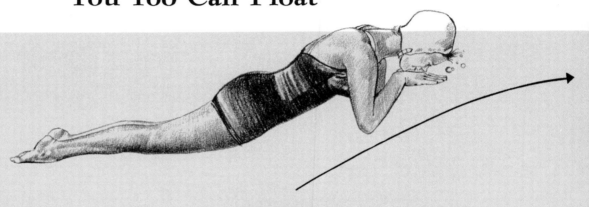

The Face Float in Shallow Water

THE ABILITY TO FLOAT is the ability to survive in the water—and the ability to swim. Sometimes nervous tension or a lack of co-ordination will make it difficult for some beginners to learn to float. And there are a few people whose small chest cavity or heavy bone structure makes it hard for them, if not impossible, to float without using a few simple paddling motions called sculling. But these people and everyone else can, with patience and practice, learn to float. Here we go.

The prone, or face, float is the basis for the crawl stroke, the breast stroke and the dog paddle. It's important for proper body position and balance in the water.

Take a position in shallow water as if you were going to do push-ups: the arms straight, supporting the body, and your legs stretched straight back. The hands should be directly beneath the shoulders.

Take a deep breath and slowly lower the face into the water to about ear depth. Your legs will

start to rise. SLOWLY bend your elbows and bring your hands together beneath your face. Then, with hands together palms down, slowly extend your arms straight out in front of your head, on the surface of the water. Your upper arms should be pressing against your ears.

Stretch your body from fingers to toes. Your legs will float faster and easier if you stretch. Hold the position for several counts.

If your body starts to roll to one side, one leg is higher than the other. Correct this and you'll float levelly. The same roll will occur if the arms are too high or two low in the water, or if the head is too high. Keep your chin on your chest and your head will be in the proper position to prevent rolling.

To get out of the prone float, slowly drop your hands to the bottom. When they're in supporting position, raise your head.

Practice the prone float until you can achieve it easily and hold it.

This is a good place to remind you again to MOVE SLOWLY. You can float. Don't panic or grope desperately for the bottom of the pool or lake. Sudden, jerky movements will only net you a mouthful of water. PRETEND YOU'RE IN SLOW MOTION.

If you find you sink below the surface, one of three things is wrong—the feet are not extended with the ankles arched, the arms are pressing down instead of extending, or the breath is not being held.

31

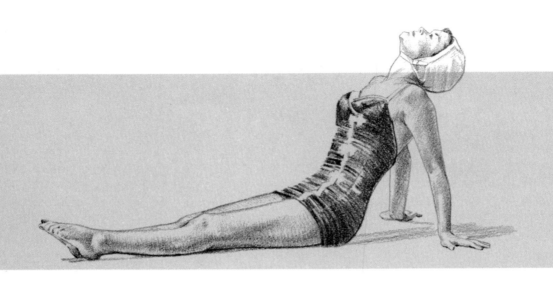

The Back Float in Shallow Water

In this position, your nose and mouth will be above the water. It will further increase your confidence in the supporting power of the water.

Sit down in shallow water. With your arms held straight, place your hands flat on the bottom of the pool or lake about two feet behind your hips and a little to each side.

Tilt your head back until your ears are under water. Keep your eyes open and look up.

Now, keeping your hands on the bottom, arch your back and lift your chest as if you were doing a back bend. You'll feel the water supporting your body, even though your feet still touch the bottom.

Keeping the head well back, very SLOWLY lift your hands from the bottom and raise them until they rest on the surface of the water, straight out from your shoulders, and you look like a letter T. Keep your arms straight and your hands and wrists relaxed.

Now your feet should begin to float up from the bottom. Keeping your chest well up and your head tilted back, straighten your legs and bring them together at the surface. Keep your legs straight, ankles arched and toes pointed. If your legs won't float when close together, extend them in a V as wide as you have to, to make them float. Or you can move your arms slowly backward, hands relaxed, to counterbalance the weight of your legs.

YOU'RE FLOATING!

If your body rolls from side to side, it's probably because one arm is too far below the surface or not in line with the shoulder. Check the arm positions and you should be all right.

In the perfect float your head stays back and your back is well arched, with the hips lifted high. Roll your head from side to side or nod front to back. You'll notice that the position of your chest and hips determines the back float.

To get out of the float, slowly drop your arms until your hands rest against the bottom of the pool. Bend at the waist and drop your hips to the bottom. Raise your head and you're back where you started.

Practice the float until you can get into it without trouble and are relaxed enough to breathe normally all the time you're floating.

The lessons on floating are very valuable to the future swimmer for purposes of resting and gaining the proper body position in the water for swimming. Therefore the floating techniques should be thoroughly mastered.

If at first you don't succeed in getting your young learners to get into floats by themselves, refer to the Teaching the Very Young section. Have the teacher assist the child into the floats as outlined there. Sometimes, if a child has initial difficulty with the face and back floats, he may have better luck with the jellyfish float and gain confidence that will help him with the others. But he must master all three floating positions before moving on.

Lesson 6

Floating in Deeper Water

AT THIS POINT, if you've mastered the last two lessons, you should feel confident that the water will support you. In the last two lessons the bottom was within an arm's length. Now we'll move into waist-deep water, where your feet alone will feel the safety of the bottom. Be sure you've mastered the earlier lessons before you move on.

The Face Float

We'll first practice getting out of the face float, to reduce the chance of any accidental duckings. In waist-deep water, take hold of the pool side or dock edge. Slowly extend your legs back on the surface of the water. Keep your legs together, instep arched and toes extended. Note that if your toes point toward the pool bottom your legs will sink. The toes must be extended backward. To stand up, slowly draw your knees to your chest, place your feet on the bottom and then slowly stand.

Try this a few times, keeping your face out of the water. Then try it with your face in the water, holding your breath. Keep your face in the water until you're ready to stand. Your face leaves the water last.

To see how your arms can help you regain your balance, stand in waist-deep water. Bend forward until your chest touches the water. Extend your arms, palms on the water, then press your arms down into the water and push them back to the surface of the water behind your hips. You'll feel the leverage they give you. Once you've done the float, I'll tell you how to use your arms in the actual recovery.

Wade out into waist-deep water. Extend your arms and lower your body by bending your knees until the water is above your shoulders. Your outstretched arms rest on the surface of the water. Hands are side by side, also resting on the surface.

Take a naturally deep breath and submerge

34

your head until your eyes, ears and nose are under the surface. Slowly and gently lean forward as if you were going to slide on top of the water. As you do, give a gentle push with your toes so that your body glides onto the water. Stretch your legs and close them as they float to the surface.

You're floating and you should glide along a few feet. REMEMBER TO AIM ACROSS THE POOL OR ALONG THE SHORE SO THAT YOU DON'T GLIDE INTO DEEPER WATER.

To stand again: Draw your knees up to your chest by bending at the hips, but don't grasp your knees with your arms. Instead, keeping your arms straight, pull them down through the water and back until they reach the surface of the water behind your hips. Keep your face submerged until you straighten your legs and touch the bottom and regain your balance.

Don't raise your head until you regain your balance. If you do, you'll only fall forward into the water. Don't spring off the bottom, for here again you'll only fall forward. As you've heard before, sudden movements will only get you into trouble. TAKE IT SLOWLY. If the movements are gentle, the reaction of the water will be slight.

Repeat the lesson until you can float easily and with no fear of the waist-deep water.

Be sure to keep your head well down as you go into and maintain the float.

Now that the learners are in deeper water, Mom and Dad want to be sure to stay close by, to make sure Junior doesn't get an accidental ducking as he comes out of a float.

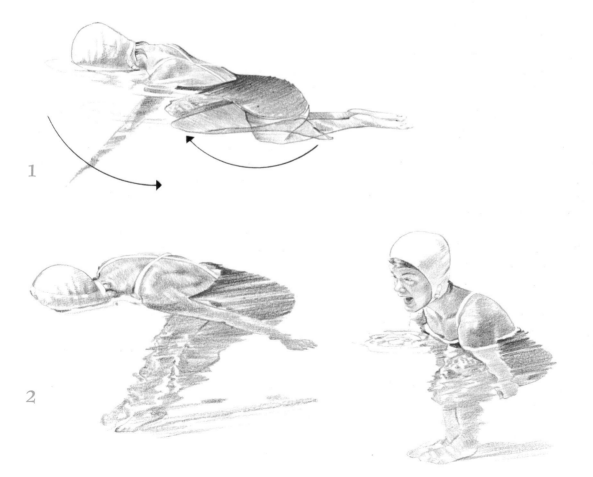

1

2

35

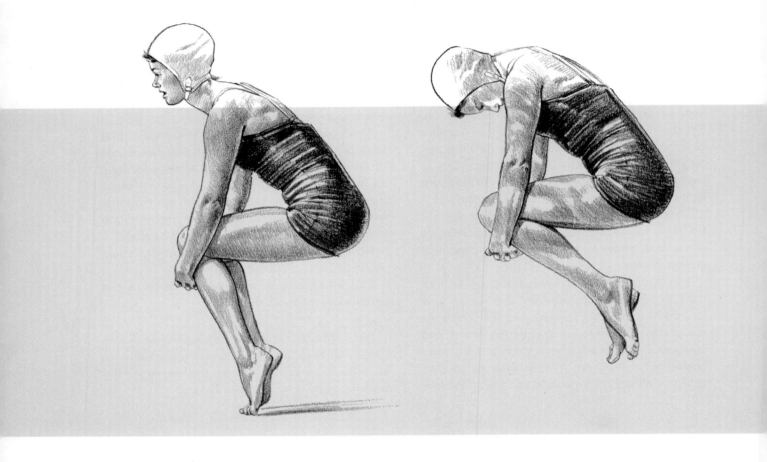

The Jellyfish Float

This is the easiest way to float. Its value to you is that it proves that water will support you.

Wade out into waist-deep water. Squat down until your chin touches the water. Clasp your hands just below the knees. Take a naturally deep breath and lower your head under the water. As your feet rise from the bottom, pull your knees up against your chest. Your chin should rest on your chest so that knees and head touch.

You're now floating. Only the middle of your back should be above the water. The motion of the water may make you roll like a fisherman's cork. It's kind of fun.

To end the float, release your knees and let your feet touch bottom again. When your feet are firmly set and you've regained your balance, straighten up. Make these movements SLOWLY, so that you don't lose your balance.

The Back Float

When you become an accomplished swimmer, you'll find that floating on your back is one of swimming's real pleasures. To dive into a lake on a hot day, swim a few yards and then roll on your back and laze there a moment or two gives a sense of ease and well-being that can't be beat. Let's learn how.

Wade out into waist-deep water. Squat until your shoulders are submerged and your chin is just out of the water. One leg should be slightly forward, the other slightly back. Extend your arms straight out from your shoulders and slightly backward. Rest your arms on the water palms down.

SLOWLY tilt your head back until your ears are under water. SLOWLY lean back and, as you do, raise your chest and lift your hips. During all this, your back stays on the surface of the water.

36

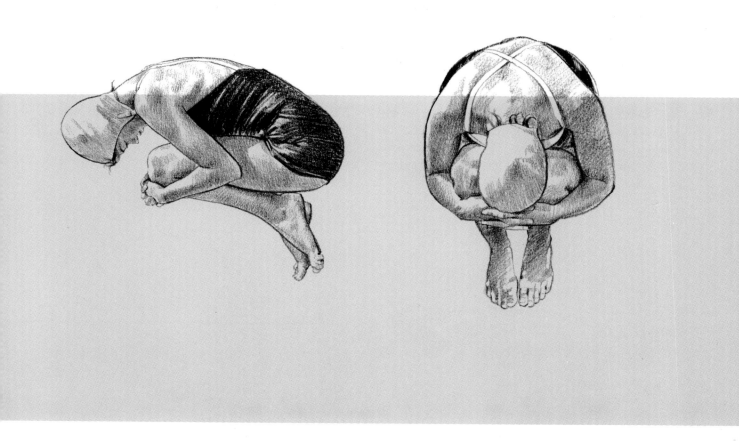

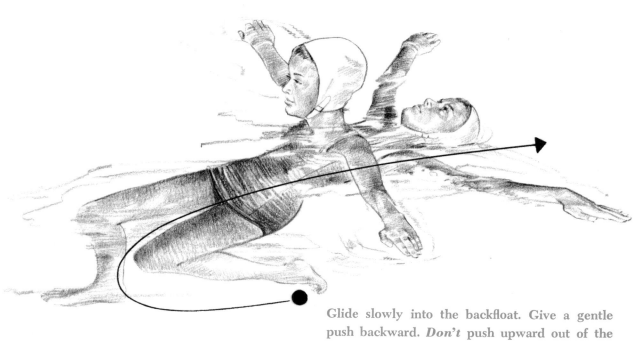

Glide slowly into the backfloat. Give a gentle push backward. *Don't* push upward out of the water.

You'll find that your body is gliding backward on the water. As it does, give a GENTLE push with the back leg and let your other leg rise to the surface. When the back leg rises, bring both legs together.

Your body will glide backward along the water. Keep your head tilted back and you can breathe normally. After practice, this position can be held for several minutes.

Getting back to a standing position from the back float in deep water may be difficult for some people. The easiest way is to go into the jellyfish float. Take a deep breath. Slowly draw up your knees to your chest by lowering your hips; bring your head forward into the water and clasp your hands around your knees. Release your knees when you're vertical and SLOWLY set your feet on the bottom. When you've regained your balance, lift your head and stand erect.

Here's another way, which is not as complicated as it sounds: Take a deep breath. Draw your knees up toward your chest. Your hips will begin to sink. As they do, bring your head and chest forward and into the water as in the jellyfish float. With your palms facing down, press your

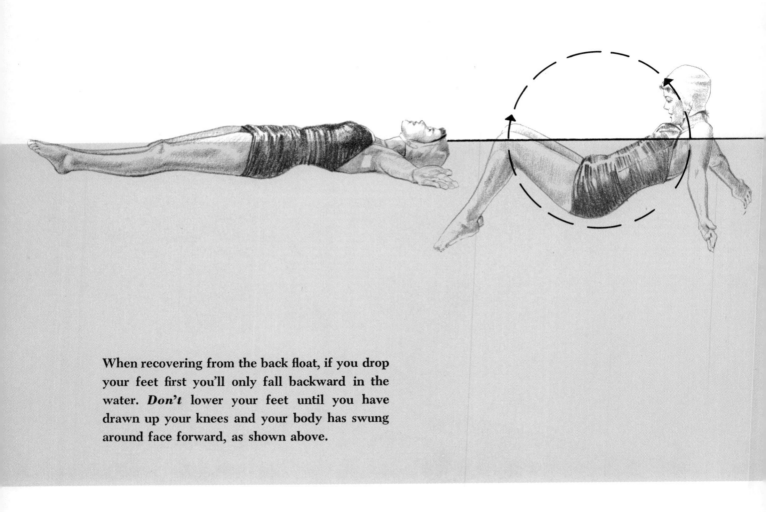

When recovering from the back float, if you drop your feet first you'll only fall backward in the water. *Don't* lower your feet until you have drawn up your knees and your body has swung around face forward, as shown above.

hands and arms straight down through the water and forward. Then, palms now facing up, with elbows close to your body, pull your hands straight up to the surface of the water in a scooping motion. This motion will have the effect of pulling your body down in the water. Your head will be under water. SLOWLY UNBEND YOUR LEGS AND SET YOUR FEET ON THE BOTTOM. When you've regained your balance, stand.

Let me repeat. Keep all your motions slow. In particular, DON'T SPRING OFF THE BOTTOM when you're getting into the back float. And don't aim

so that you'll be gliding into deep water.

If you find you're one of the people who have a hard time floating, see the next lesson.

It's especially important here that Dad demonstrate how to get out of the back float. On his own, the child's inclination may be to roll over, and if he does he'll end up with a mouthful and some uneasy moments.

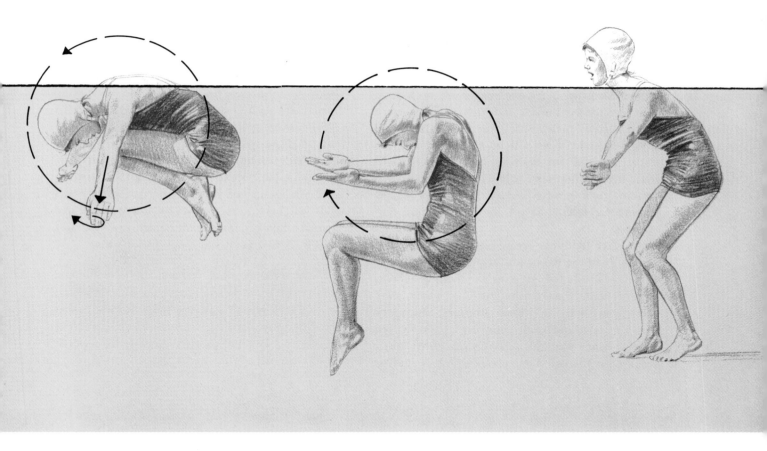

39

The Handy Art of Sculling

THIS LESSON is primarily for people who don't float easily, and it's a particularly good technique for anyone trying to float in rough water. Sculling is a simple paddling motion which increases your floating power.

Get into a back float as in Lesson 5. Here's how, briefly: Sit in shallow water, arms straight and your hands touching bottom about two feet behind each hip. Tilt your head back, arch your back and lift your chest and hips as if you were doing a back bend. Lift your hands from the bottom and let them rest on the surface of the water, straight out from your shoulders. Hold your legs straight and together and point your toes by arching your insteps. Your legs should have started to float. If not, they will as you begin sculling.

Now for sculling. Bring your arms to your thighs. Turn the palms out and gently push your arms outward ten to twelve inches, elbows slightly bent. Here you're pushing water away from your body. Without stopping, turn the palms inward and push your arms back to your body, elbows straight. Your hands don't quite touch your thighs. What you're doing is making

a gentle figure-eight motion with your hands. Keep your wrists, arms and hands relaxed. Palms out as you push out, palms in as you push in. Your hands should be about six inches below the surface of the water.

Just this little motion is enough to keep a poor floater afloat, head out of water.

Now that we've taken up sculling, here's a third way to recover from the back-float position: In the back-float position, let your body jackknife slightly so that your hips drop. As you do this, start sculling gently and bring your chest forward. Still sculling to maintain balance, let your feet touch the bottom. Don't attempt to stand up until you're sure of your balance; otherwise you may fall back into the water. As with all recoveries, take a deep breath before you start and hold it. It may save you a noseful of water.

Most children, and indeed most swimmers, won't need to know sculling as an aid to floating. But it's an invaluable part of skills we'll be learning later, like treading water, and so mastering the simple arm motion right here is well worth while.

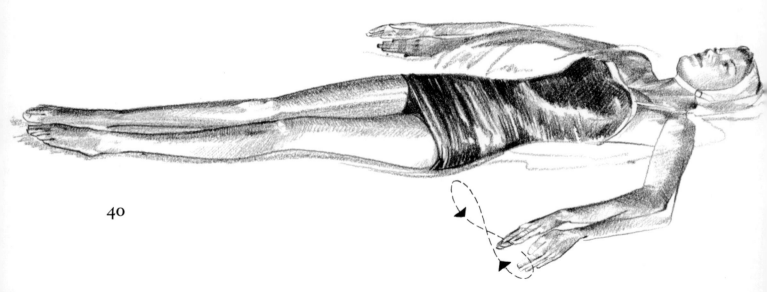

Lesson 8

Flat on Your Back, Floating and Kicking

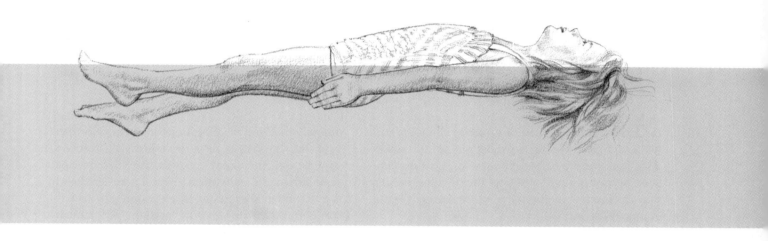

By now you should be floating as easily as a veteran trout. So we'll add another ingredient and move a step closer to actual swimming.

In waist-deep water, go into a back float. Make sure that your back is arched as high as it will go, to get your chest and your hips well up in the water. Now slowly bring your arms to your sides, sculling a little if you need to, to keep afloat on an even keel. Place your palms against your thighs. Arch your head well back (keep your eye on the sky or the ceiling). Your ears should be under water but your nose and mouth exposed so that you can breathe naturally.

Start kicking. Make it a slow waltz: one-two-three, one-two-three. The three-beat kicking rhythm keeps you from favoring one leg and moving in circles. Remember again, stay parallel to the shore or the short length of the pool so that you're not heading into deep water. Breathe normally through your mouth.

Don't be in a hurry to get to a standing position. Stop kicking and let your movement through the water come almost to a stop. Sculling gently, slowly drop your hips, bring your chest forward and lower your feet to the bottom. When your feet are firmly set, stand up. Easy does it. Now try the whole procedure again.

Lesson 9

The Dog Paddle, of All Things

MOST FOLKS learning to swim by the slow and painful trial-and-error method at the old swimmin' hole (and whatever became of the old swimmin' hole, anyway?) discover the dog paddle. It's the instinctive method by which animals—and humans—swim.

And it's the way we're going to start, too. For my money, the dog paddle is the "life stroke." The simple ability to dog-paddle has saved many lives, and will save many more.

The paddle itself is a natural, uncomplicated motion that doesn't need much explaining. Try to imagine that you're going to pedal a tricycle with your hands. When your right arm is stretched straight out and starts to press, your left arm is doubled up close to your body and your left hand is just under your chin. When your left arm is straight and starting the press, your right hand is just under your chin. Paddling isn't exactly like pedaling, but it will give you an idea of the relationship of your arms. Study the drawing. In the stroke, your arm reaches straight out, then presses downward until it points straight at the bottom. Then you bend your elbow, keeping the

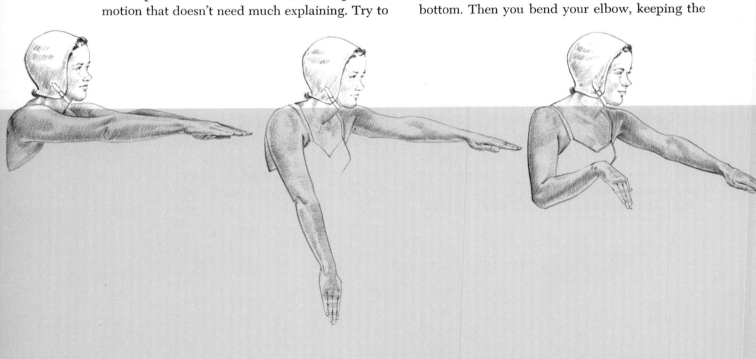

upper arm close to the body, and raise the fore-arm so that the hand comes just below the surface in front of the chest, below the chin.

Try the paddling first on dry land, then standing in waist-deep water, leaning forward with your chest on the water. Remember these points:

1. Both arms remain under water all the time.
2. Your elbows stay close to your body, not out to the side.
3. At the top of its cycle, the arm stretches full out.
4. Keep your elbows low on recovery.

Now let's try it for real. Take a deep breath and go into a prone (face-down) float in shallow water. Start kicking, letting your knees bend more than you normally would. Now start paddling. Paddle and kick as long as you can. You're holding your breath, so it won't be for long. Since you're in shallow water, when you're out of breath just put your hands on the bottom and lift your face out of the water.

Repeat this several times, now starting in waist-deep water and paddling toward shore or the shallow end of the pool.

When you're sure you've got the hang of it,

start water breathing as you learned in Lesson 2. Go into a prone float and start kicking. As you slide your left arm forward, turn your face to the right, inhale, and, as the left arm presses down, immediately start exhaling. Turn your face down into the water as you slide your right arm forward.

You're swimming!

After a few repeats of this technique, try going into a prone float, lifting your head out of the water and breathing through your mouth. Then paddle away to your heart's content.

One small point to remember: With the dog paddle, you should do what is called a slow flutter kick, bending the knees more than in the regular thrash described in Lesson 3.

Young swimmers and, in fact, many swimmers may find it easier to dog paddle with their heads out of water before they try combining the dog paddle with water breathing. The water breathing is, of course, a necessity in the crawl to come, but let them start here with whichever is easiest. As you noted in Part One, I skip water breathing for the small fry.

Starting to Crawl—
The Arm Stroke

You now have all the elements for the American crawl—breathing, kicking, floating—except the arm stroke. Now, just before we take up the stroke, I'm going to introduce you to a new swimming term.

The term is *recovery*. It refers to that part of the arm motion in which the arm, having delivered its power, returns to begin a new stroke. In the crawl, the arm goes down through the water, describing perhaps two thirds of a circle. Then, having delivered its power, it swings out and across the water and down to begin a new stroke. That's the recovery.

The arm stroke is, obviously, all-important in good swimming, so we'll study it in some detail.

How the Stroke Works

Wade into waist-deep water. Bending your knees a little, lean over from the waist so that your chest just touches the water. Place your

How one arm looks making the power stroke (press, pull, push) and the straight-arm recovery. Arm is straight but relaxed, not stiff. Don't pull shoulder forward by overreaching.

arms in front of you, side by side and palms down, on the surface of the water. Imagine that your arms are resting on a table top. As you do, notice three things:

1. The hands are neither cupped downward nor tilted up from the wrists;
2. The hands are not sharply twisted at the wrists, but
3. The hand, in a natural relaxed position, tends to turn slightly toward the body. Many beginners introduce an unnatural twisting or cupping of the hands. Remember the table top and you'll avoid these faults.

Leave one arm extended on the surface of the water. *Press* the other arm straight down into the water, *pull* it through the water and *push* it back toward the thigh. Your thumb should lightly graze your thigh. At the hip, your hand is about six inches below the water. This completes the power part of the stroke. Now the recovery.

Think of your arm as an oar, with your shoulder as the oarlock. Raise your shoulder and arm from the water, bend your elbow SLIGHTLY. Bring your arm to a position straight out from the shoulder and swing it in a low, wide arc across the water to a position alongside your other arm.

Note well that your arm does not go straight up in the air like the blade of a windmill. Instead, it travels much more nearly horizontally to the surface of the water. Your hand should be at most eight to ten inches above the water.

Try the stroke again with the same arm (the arm should enter the water gently). *Press* straight down into the water; *pull* through the water and *push* your arm back until the thumb grazes the hip. Swing your arm out of the water, to the side and forward. Practice until you can do it smoothly.

Analyzing the Stroke

As you've noticed from my description, the arm stroke has three distinct muscular parts, although they go together so smoothly that the swimmer is apt not to be aware of them. From the surface to about a foot below the surface, the arm *presses*.

The straight-arm recovery. Note that the hand and arm do not twist and that the arm travels nearly horizontally to the water, not more than 10 inches above the surface. Keep your eyes open to watch the press-pull-push of the power stroke.

Then the arm *pulls* until it's vertical or straight down in the water. Then it *pushes* back to the hip. The importance of the analysis is this: By giving an extra effort to the *push,* good swimmers can get an extra thrust.

Note also that as the arm recovers from the water the hand does not rotate independently. Rather, the arm turns the hand so that the hand faces the surface of the water as it enters.

Practice the stroke with each arm separately, until the motion is smooth and continuous.

Straight-Arm vs. Bent-Arm Recovery

What I have described here is called the straight-arm stroke and recovery. As you noticed, the arm bends, but only slightly. There is also what is called the bent-arm recovery. Here, once the straight arm has delivered its power, the elbow bends considerably for the recovery. I've been teaching the straight-arm recovery for the American crawl for thirty years. At first, most other coaches taught the bent-arm recovery, but during the last few years my method—the straight-arm recovery—has found increasing popularity. Today many national and world swimming champions, both men and women, use the straight-arm stroke.

I feel that *all* beginning swimmers should use the straight-arm stroke and recovery, even though some of them may eventually come to prefer the bent-arm recovery. If they do, well and good. But starting out with the bent-arm recovery, I have found, often introduces an unnatural twisting of the arms and hands during the stroke and makes for less efficient swimming because there is a tendency to shorten the power part of the stroke. If you learn the straight-arm stroke properly, you'll do the bent-arm stroke better if you decide to adopt it later on. We'll discuss the bent-arm recovery at greater length in Chapter 23. For now, believe me, you'll do better to stay with the straight-arm recovery.

What is important is that they now develop the correct straight-arm recovery. Dad should demonstrate the correct stroke in slow motion, emphasizing the *press* down, the *pull* through, the *push* back and the sweeping recovery. He should take the child's arm and steer it through the stroke. The youngsters should study the drawings carefully. Patient striving for perfection here will pay dividends forever after in graceful, efficient swimming.

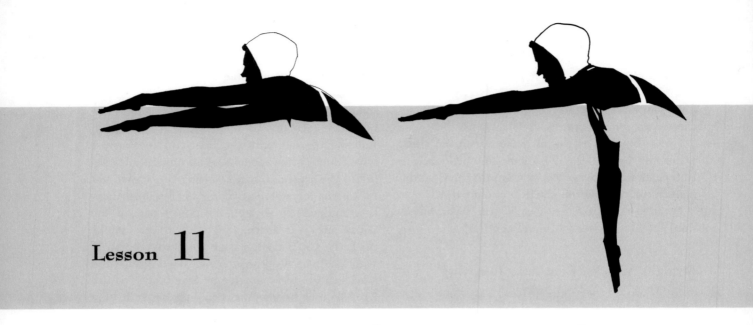

Lesson 11

Putting Both Arms to Work

WHEN YOU'VE MASTERED the correct arm motions for each arm, try putting them together. Like this:

As in Lesson 10, wade into waist-deep water and bend over until your chest just touches the water. Extend your arms before you on the surface of the water, hands together, palms down.

With the *right* arm, start the press down through the water. As the *right* hand approaches the thigh in its push, the *left* arm begins its press down through the water. As the *left* arm pulls down, the *right* starts its recovery over the water.

As the left arm approaches the thigh, or starts its push, the *right* starts the press down of its own stroke.

Repeat the strokes until they're smooth. The arms should perform an even, continuous motion with no hesitation. At this point don't try for speed; try instead to make the motions graceful, not only for looks but for easier, smoother swimming.

Points to remember: Your thumbs should

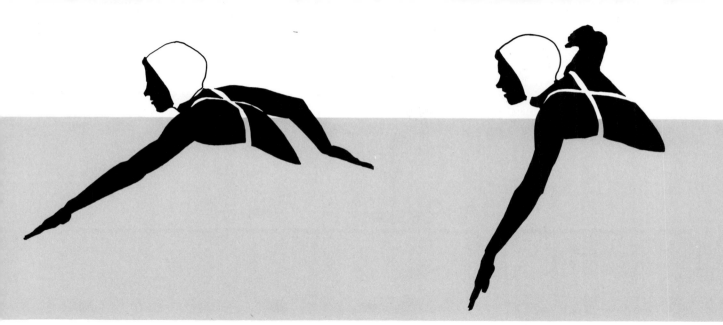

lightly graze your thighs at the end of the power stroke. Doing this will assure you that you're drawing your arm straight down through the water for maximum power. On the recovery, remember the oar image and swing your arm wide over the water, not straight up in the air.

Now let's try the arm motion with the head in the water, feet on the bottom.

Take the same position as before, with your chest just touching the water. Take a deep breath, hold it, and slowly lower your head into the water. The water should come to your brow line and to the front of your ears. Remember to keep your head parallel to the water, as if you were looking straight into a mirror.

With your head motionless in the water, stroke for as long as you can easily hold your breath—and at least for several complete strokes. Rest; then try it again. Make the arm motions slow, smooth and graceful.

Note well that the arm motion should *not* change once the head is lowered into the water. In fact, the motion may seem easier because having the head in the water eases strain on the neck muscles.

The youngsters may be rarin' to get on with the "real" swimming, but it's important to practice the stroke in place so that it becomes mechanical. That way it will take care of itself when we come to combine it with floating, kicking and breathing.

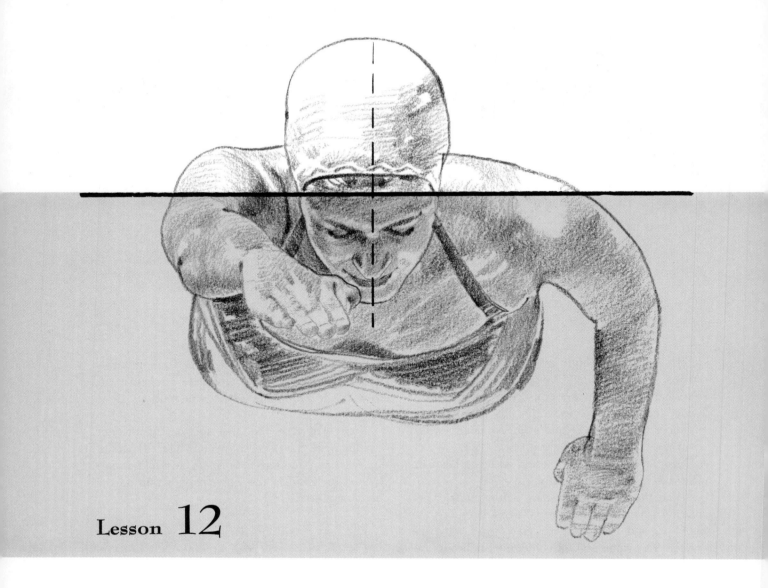

Almost There—
Arms in Motion While You Float

Wɪᴛʜ ᴛʜɪs ʟᴇssᴏɴ we're going beyond the dog paddle and for the first time doing a rudimentary kind of arms-above-water swimming. Here we'll try it for very short distances, holding the breath. In the next lesson we'll try it holding the head out of water. Finally we'll put all three elements— kicking, stroke and breathing—together.

Take and hold a deep breath and go into a face or prone float, with your face in the water and your arms outstretched on the water, as you did in Lesson 6.

Start kicking, slowly and evenly. Mentally count your kicks. After three kicks or so, start the arm motion.

50

EACH FULL ARM STROKE—FROM THE TIME THE ARM STARTS ITS PRESS THROUGH THE WATER UNTIL IT'S READY TO PRESS AGAIN—LASTS SIX COUNTS, OR KICKS.

On *one*, the arm starts its press down. On *two*, it's in the pull. At *three* the hand is at the thigh. Now, instead of counting *four, five* and *six* for the recovery over the water, which completes the arm stroke, we'll count *one, two* and *three* for the power stroke in the other arm. The recovery, mastered in the last lesson, will take care of itself without having to be counted.

So the count goes one-two-three, one-two-three. You can, if you prefer, say press-pull-push, press-pull-push. Remember that while you're giving three counts for one arm the other arm is executing its recovery over the water.

At first you may feel—as I've noted before—as you did if you ever tried to pat the top of your head and rub your stomach at the same time. With practice, however, it should come easily.

There may, on the other hand, be those who can't think about their arms and their legs at the same time. For these folks—and as further practice for anyone—try these variations:

1. Count your arm motion, as I've indicated above, but forget about co-ordinating your kick. Count one-two-three as your arm makes its press-pull-push through the water. Keep kicking steadily, but at this point don't worry about whether or not you're doing six kicks for each *complete* arm stroke.

2. Then forget about your arms and count your kicks, again on the three-count cycle. For example: *one* (right foot down), *two* (left foot down), *three* (right foot down). Don't attempt to co-ordinate the arm motion with your kick. Concentrate on your kick timing and simply do the arm strokes the most natural way. Perfection comes when the arms and legs move in the same rhythm, six kicks equaling one *complete* arm stroke.

Switch back and forth, counting sometimes the kicks, sometimes the arm strokes. Eventually you'll find that your arms and legs are making the proper co-ordination. If anyone is watching you and attempting to analyze your motions, his job will be made easier, because jerky or improper kick or arm motions will show up quickly when you're concentrating on one or the other.

Remember that at first we're trying this with the head in the water, so you'll be able to do only two or three strokes. Rest after each attempt so that you don't get winded.

Let your young swimmers just kick and stroke the first few times, without worrying about the count. Eventually, of course, they must acquire the counting. A swimmer can be compared to a car, the various parts of which must work together in co-ordinated rhythm in order for it to ride smoothly and powerfully. Counting provides the rhythm that helps the swimmer's body, arms and legs work together. When the rhythm is right, the swimmer purrs along like an aquatic Cadillac.

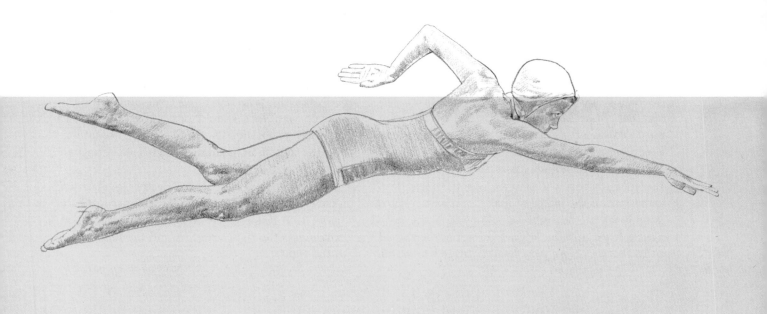

Lesson 13

Swimming!

WE'RE NOW READY to swim longer distances. Breathing will be through the mouth, with the head held above water. But the head will describe much the same motion it does in underwater breathing.

Go into a prone float, as in the last lesson, with the hands outstretched in front of the body and together. Start kicking, but instead of lowering the head into the water hold it high enough to keep your mouth above the surface.

Start the arm motion, again as in the last lesson. But now there's a difference. As the *right* arm comes out of the water to make its recovery, turn your head to the right as if to watch the arm Your left ear and the left side of your face should be in the water. As your head is turned to watch

your arm swing over, inhale through your mouth. Immediately start to exhale through slightly compressed lips. At the same time, lift your chin slightly and turn your head to the front.

Now your left arm lifts from the water to start its recovery. As it does, turn your head to the left to watch the arm. Your right ear and the right side of your face should now lie in the water. Continue to exhale. The head doesn't hesitate as it turns and it immediately begins its return to the right side.

The right arm leaves the water to start its recovery. Turn your head to the right and inhale again. Your timing must be so that you've finished exhaling as the right arm lifts and the head turns to the right.

52

With each stroke, the head turns to watch the arm's recovery. However, THE BREATH IS INHALED ON ONE SIDE ONLY. Now, I've said above that you should inhale on the right side. Most swimmers do. It actually makes no difference, and many swimmers (interestingly enough, it's most often left-handed people), find it more natural to breathe on the left side. If you find you're a left-sided breather, go to it. The thing to remember is to breathe *on one side only*.

As you swim, remember that the motion of the head· is just about continuous. Remember also that at no point is the breath held. You breathe in on one side, immediately start exhaling and keep exhaling until the head returns to the original side position and you draw a new breath.

You're now putting a lot of lessons together. As you swim increasingly greater distances, check yourself on these points:

1. The top of the head should point in the direction in which you're swimming. If it's cocked to one side, you'll veer in that direction.

2. The hands should not be cupped or bent up at the wrists, but should be flat, like the blade of an oar.

3. The shoulder should *not* dip into the water on the stroke. Many beginners try to reach too deep into the water, thinking they'll get more power. It doesn't work out that way.

4. Remember the press-pull-push sequence of the stroke. It will help in your timing and smooth-ness. Pull your arms *straight* down and back.

5. Don't try for speed. At this stage, SMOOTH-NESS AND TIMING are all-important. Count your kicking and be sure your stroke is on the six-kick cycle.

As you swim greater distances, you'll·notice the strain on your neck muscles. That's why, for real distance swimming, the head-in-water breathing technique we practiced in Lesson 2 is the only answer. It all but eliminates the strain on the neck muscles.

Before going on to the next lesson, review Lesson 2, practicing breathing in the standing position.

If you find it too difficult to swim with your head up, skip this chapter and go on to the next, which teaches underwater breathing. Then, if you like, come back to this chapter.

For most beginners, learning first with the head out of water makes it far easier to master the breathing technique. This approach also helps the beginner decide whether he is better suited to right-side or left-side breathing.

This is a particularly good time to give your young pupils a kind of mid-term rest, a few days of practice to let the skills learned so far soak in, as I suggested early in the book. Right now, before we tackle the true American crawl, Dad should watch critically and see that the young-sters' kick, stroke and timing are letter-perfect.

Mastering the American Crawl

In this lesson, for the sake of clarity, I'm going to refer to the right side as the breathing side. But, as I indicated in the last lesson, you can breathe on either side so long as you breathe on one side only while you're learning.

We'll now combine breathing and the stroke, practicing in place first. Standing in waist-deep water, bend forward with your chest on the water and your arms extended forward. Slowly start the arm stroke, with your head out of the water. Do two or three strokes this way. Then, as your right arm starts its push back through the water, turn your head to the right. As your right arm lifts out of the water, inhale through the mouth. As the arm swings forward, turn your head into the water, exhaling through the nose and the slightly compressed lips the way you learned previously. Practice, standing in place, until you've mastered this co-ordination of breathing and arm stroke.

Go into a prone float, start kicking, and swim a few strokes with the head out of water as you did in the last lesson.

Now, as the head turns to the right to watch the arm's recovery, take a breath. But this time, instead of keeping the head above water and turning to the front, lower the face into the water, as you've practiced. Breathing is continuous. You inhale and then immediately start exhaling. The exhaling—through both the nose and the slightly compressed lips, remember—continues as the face turns to point straight at the bottom, continues as the head turns again to the right and as the right arm begins its push back. The nose and mouth break above water as the right arm lifts out of the water and makes its recovery.

Some learners may have found it impossible to swim with the head out of the water, as described in the previous chapter. These people should go into a prone float, start kicking and take two or three strokes with the face in the water. Then, as the right arm starts its push back through the water, turn the head to the right. As the right arm lifts from the water, inhale and go into the breathing sequence as practiced at the start of this chapter.

The head should be submerged slightly above the eyebrows. If the head is held too low in the water, the swimmer cannot get his mouth high enough for air and he swallows water. He'll tend to jerk his head out of the water. If the head is held too high in the water, it will interfere with the arm recovery and also increase the strain on the neck muscles. It may help if you remember the imaginary pillow of water. Your head lies on it as you turn to the right to watch the arm recovery and inhale, and your face is buried in it as you turn to the *center*. Remember also, even if it seems unflattering, the idea of your head's being an orange jammed on the end of a stick. Your neck and spine (the stick) stay relatively straight and only your head swivels, right to center and back, like the orange.

Your breathing cycle and kick beat are timed to your arm stroke. The importance, first, of continuous, rhythmical kicking and, second, of smooth, continuous breathing should now be clear.

Perhaps the most difficult part of swimming, at this stage, is controlling the breathing cycle so that your lungs are completely emptied just at the moment your nose and mouth break out of the water. Remember that exhaling starts immediately after you've taken a breath. You should be exhaling even before your nose and mouth dip under the surface again, to prevent water from entering. Don't expel the air too forcibly. You'll tend to blow all the air out at once and to acquire the bad habit of holding your breath.

You're now a swimmer, and I hope a graceful one. From now on, the more you practice, the better and more graceful swimmer you'll become.

In the rest of this book we'll take up the other swimming strokes, diving and some more tips that will help make you the master of the water.

For a guide to how well your children are doing, here are some rough standards. Recently I had one student who, at age six, could swim twenty laps of the pool. He's exceptional; an average six-year-old should be able to swim perhaps three or four hundred yards. An eight-year-old should do a thousand yards, a ten-year-old a mile.

But let me remind you that children (like adults) can overestimate their swimming ability. Kids should never be in the water without responsible supervision. And, wherever they're swimming, there should be clear-cut and well-understood safety rules. These should include swimming parallel to the shore or to the end of the pool and knowing where the deep water is. The old rule about giving your digestion a chance and not swimming for an hour after meals is still in force, too.

1

Here, in a ten-drawing sequence, is how breathing and arm motion are synchronized through one complete stroke.

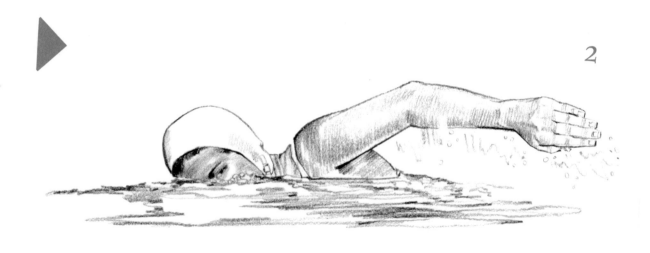

2

3

4

56

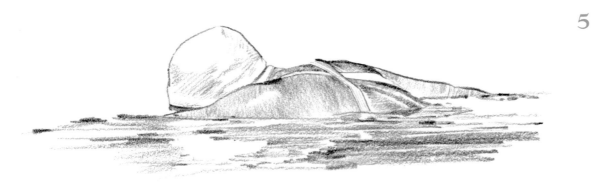

5

6

7

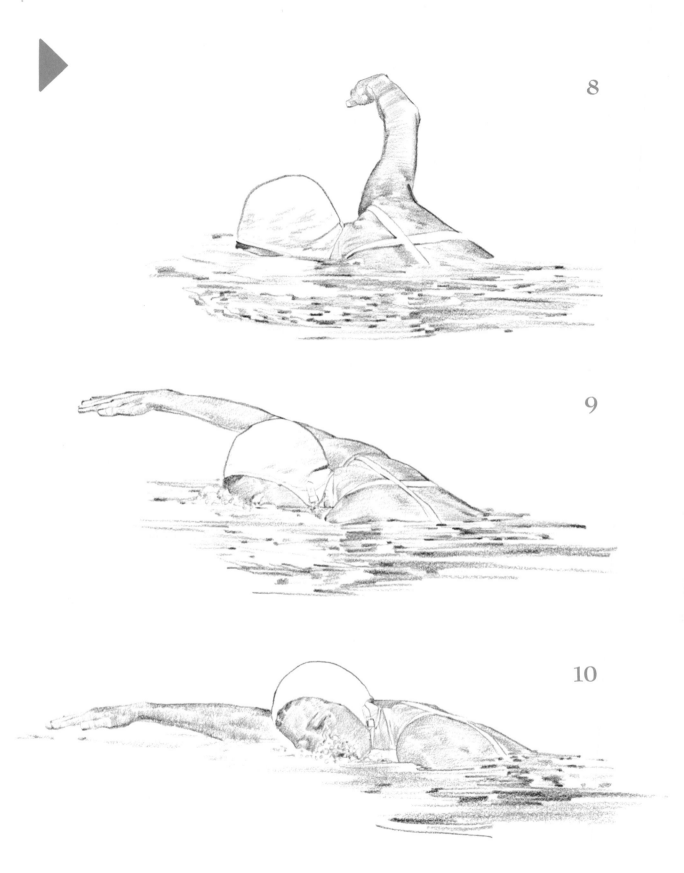

8

9

10

Part Three

DIVES, MORE STROKES
AND OTHER WATERY JOYS

THE SWIMMER has now mastered the basic stroke, the one he'll use more than any other. But the fun has really only begun. We'll now consider, briefly, the useful art of getting into the water. Then we'll take up the other strokes. (A swimmer who knew only one stroke would find life as dull and limited as a pianist who knew only "Humoresque.") These strokes are, of course, useful as well as pleasurable. We'll learn them, as we did the crawl, by perfecting the component parts and then putting them together.

Children should learn simple dives and treading water (Lesson 20) as soon as possible. The other strokes are optional, to be mastered when their abilities and interest indicate. The descriptions of those strokes, incidentally, occasionally sound formidable. They aren't, but I've spelled them out in detail for complete accuracy. Study the text in close connection with the drawings. Even long-time swimmers may well find helpful pointers in these lessons.

Easy Dives

Diving—championship or exhibition diving—is an art and is beyond the scope of this book. But once you've become a good swimmer, able to handle yourself in the water, you're ready to end the tedium of wading out into the water or clambering down the pool ladder. You're ready to make simple dives into the water, and that's what we'll take up here.

First, a few cautions. An experienced diver *can* make a successful flat dive into relatively shallow water, but this is extremely hazardous for anyone, and especially for the beginning diver. Practice these dives—and all your early dives—in

water that is over your head. Never dive unless you've checked the depth of the water and have made sure that there are no submerged or hidden rocks, pilings or debris which you might strike.

Jumping Feet First

To begin, let's try a feet-first jump. Stand at the edge of the pool or dock with body straight and arms held straight at the sides. Take and hold a breath, bend your knees and spring out into the water, keeping your body relatively straight. When your feet hit bottom, bend your knees to absorb the shock and push up to the surface. Go into a crawl and head for shore or the ladder.

Diving from a Sitting Position

We'll work our way into head-first diving gradually, beginning from a sitting position. If you're at a pool, sit at the edge and put your feet on the gutter around the pool. If you're on a dock, you may be able to brace your feet on the dock's supporting plank. If neither is available you'll have to skip this step.

Sitting at the poolside or dock edge, lock your thumbs, palms down as in the face float, so that your hands are close together. Extend your arms straight over your head, close to your ears. Without hunching or rounding your shoulders, bend forward from the waist. Lean forward so that the hands point to the water and your body is at a forty-five-degree angle. Slowly lean farther forward. Just as you begin to lose your balance and fall forward, take and hold a deep breath and

gently push yourself away from the gutter with your feet. Straighten your legs and lift them slightly. Arch your hips slightly. Be sure to keep your head down so that the top of your head and not your face breaks the surface of the water.

Your hands, head, shoulders, hips and feet enter the water in that order. Your body should go two to three feet below the surface and glide from three to ten feet. How strongly you push away from the poolside will determine how far you glide, and the angle at which you enter the water will determine how deep you go.

Hold your body position until your body glides up to the surface. Practice this dive just a few times. Checkpoints: Be sure to keep your head down, legs straight and hips slightly arched.

Diving from a Kneeling Position

This time kneel at the edge of the pool or dock, with one foot at the edge, the other knee about twelve inches back from the edge. Lock your

thumbs, straighten your arms and point them toward the water. Bend your head down between your arms. Lean forward and, just as you start to fall, give a gentle push with your foot. As you head for the water, straighten and stretch your legs back and arch the hips as before. Glide through the water and back to the surface as you did before. Remember to keep your head down. Be sure your lower legs don't bend up from the knees. Your body should enter the water straight except for the slight arching of the hips. If you dive too flatly the water can give you a painful slap; if the body is bent too much you may even touch bottom with your head.

The Standing Dive

Before you tackle the standing dive, take time to study the pictures carefully and think your way through the action. Standing on the dock, imagine yourself in the air heading into the water. Get a mental picture of your finger pointing to the water like an arrowhead, your head tucked down between your arms, your legs straight and

your toes pointed back, with ankles arched. Good diving requires practice and there is no substitute for it. You can make a good beginning by mentally telling your body, so to speak, what it's going to do.

Stand on the side of the pool. Curl your toes over the edge of the pool, feet together. Bend your knees and bend your body from the waist at an angle of about forty-five degrees. Point your arms at the water, thumbs locked and hands (palms toward the water) flat. Lean forward and, as you begin to lose your balance, push off with your feet. Straighten your legs and raise them slightly and arch your hips. Your entry into the water should be smooth and should lead to a gentle, arching glide down into the water and then back to the surface.

The checkpoints again: Head down, body gently arched at the hips but otherwise straight. Don't bend your body after pushing off from the side of the pool. Never dive without having your arms over your head; this is important protection for the head. Be sure the water is deep.

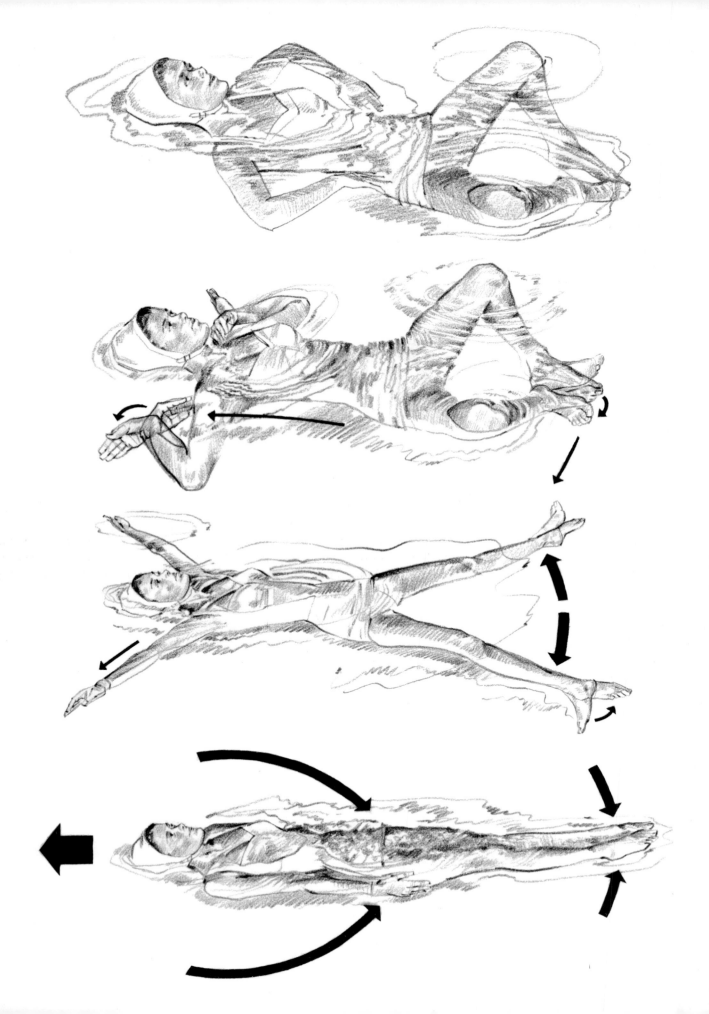

The Simple, or Elementary, Backstroke

THIS IS NOT the regulation backstroke used in competition. Instead, it's an elementary version that's easier and more restful. It's a "safety stroke," because it lets a tired swimmer rest and yet make headway in the water.

The Arms

Unlike the crawl, in which the arms apply their power alternately, in the elementary backstroke the arms work together. The effect is a little bit like a bird flapping its wings.

Go into a back float. Be sure that the body is stretched out full length and the back arched high to get the chest (but not the stomach) high in the water.

Extend the arms straight out to the side. Stretch them slightly back so that the arms are a bit farther back than shoulder level. Now lower the arms about two or three inches below the surface of the water. Here the stroke starts.

Keeping your arms straight, hands facing thighs, pull them through the water—parallel to the surface—until your hands touch your sides. The hands should be vertical in the water, like the blades of oars. As you finish the stroke, glide for two or three seconds. Keep the head well back and the chest up. The body should stay in perfect floating position through the entire stroke. No water should get on the face.

Now the recovery. Bend your elbows out so that you can bring your hands up the sides of your body with a very relaxed motion until your finger tips touch your shoulders. At that point your elbows form a straight line from the right elbow across the top of your chest to the left elbow. Turn the wrists outward and once again extend the arms full length outward and you're back to a floating position. Remember, your arms stay in the water throughout the stroke.

Begin a new stroke by pulling your arms through the water to your sides. Pause here and glide. When you've completed the power stroke, hold your arms at your sides and glide. The whole point of this stroke is that it's slow, sliding and restful. Keep your eyes open and your head well back.

You INHALE during the recovery, as your hands are moving up your body toward your shoulders. You EXHALE as you begin the armstroke through the water.

The Legs—The Frog Kick

The kick for the elementary backstroke is in three parts, or counts:

One: Slowly make a diamond shape by keeping the feet together as you bend your knees out (*not up*); the soles of the feet should be facing. Keep your feet relaxed.

Two: Slowly spread the legs apart in a wide V.

Three: Bring the legs together in a fast, whipping motion, not too hard or jerky. This is the driving force of the kick.

The counts are not even. The whipping movement is somewhat quicker than the other two. When the legs come together, pause and glide for two or three seconds.

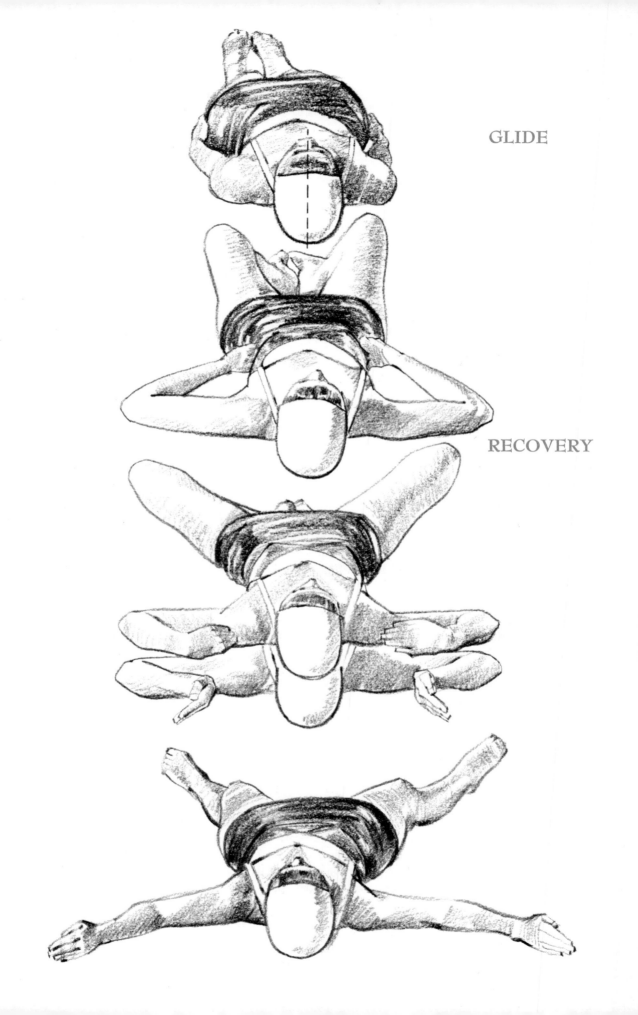

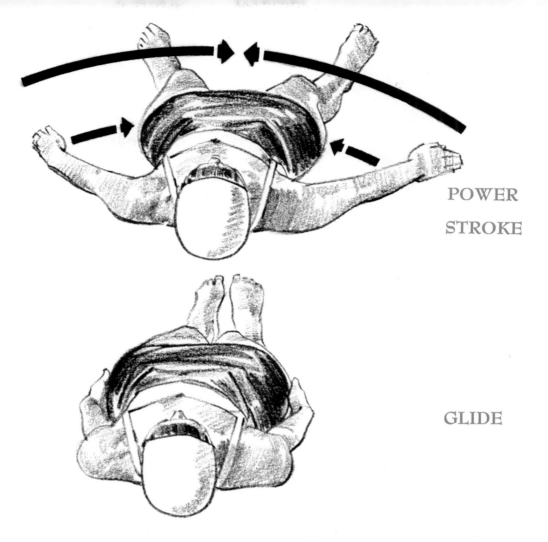

To practice it, go into a back float with the arms at the sides and the legs outstretched. Keeping the feet together, bend the knees out. Don't bend at the waist or hips. Turn the ankles outward, so that the toes also point outward. Spread your legs as far as you can to form the V. Then bring the legs together in a whipping motion. As the legs come together, the ankles are arched and the toes are extended. Keep the legs straight. Only the toes should touch. Again make the diamond shape by bending the knees outward, spread the legs and whip them together. Work for smoothness. With just the kick, you should be able to cover some distance easily.

Arms and Legs Together

It's simple and logical. As your legs are whipping together, your arms are pulling through the water. Arms and legs provide their thrust at the same time.

Take a back-float position with arms at the sides. As you bend your knees outward and bring your legs into a diamond shape, your elbows are bending and your hands move along the sides of your body to your shoulder. As your legs spread in a wide V, your arms are stretching out to the sides.

Then whip your legs together gently and at the same time pull your arms through the water to your sides. Glide for two or three seconds (you should travel two yards or so).

Practice until your arms and legs work smoothly together.

Remember the breathing technique: Inhale on the recovery, exhale on the stroke. Breathing is an important part of the exercise of this stroke.

One advantage of the backstroke is that Dad can explain what he's doing while he's doing it—and he should.

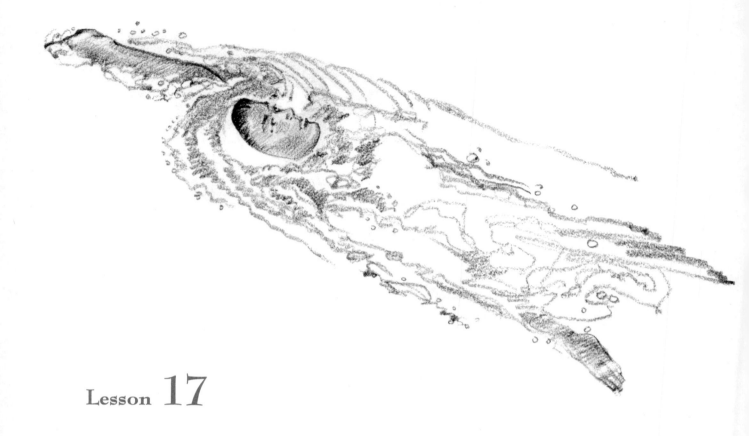

Lesson 17

The Genuine Backstroke

THIS IS THE BACKSTROKE used in competition. Aside from competition, the backstroke is dandy if you're trying to keep your eye on an airplane while swimming, or to suntan your chest, or to impress your friends.

The backstroke is sometimes called the inverted or upside-down crawl, and that's a reasonably accurate description. The kick is roughly the same one you learned for the crawl. The timing for the arm stroke is roughly the same as in the crawl. The arm motion, however, is significantly different. In the crawl, the arm pull is vertical—straight down through the water. In the backstroke, the arm pull is horizontal through the water. In the recovery over the water, the arm is halfway between the horizontal and the vertical. The reason is that moving your arms vertically (or nearly vertically) under water on your back causes the body to roll from side to side and to lift at least partly above the water, thus slowing you down.

The Kick

The leg action for the backstroke is approximately the same as for the crawl. The big difference is that most of the power in the kick comes from the upward thrust of the ankles. The knees

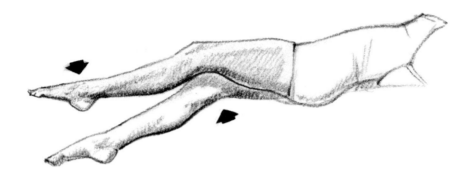

are slightly more relaxed, which causes the feet to sink slightly deeper into the water. There's good reason for this. The more water you disturb with your kicking, the more thrust you get. Floating on your back, your legs tend to be nearer the surface—too near the surface for maximum power. By relaxing your knees and letting your ankles and feet sink a little deeper into the water, you disturb more water as you kick up and you get more power. Honest! On the other hand, if the legs are too low in the water, the kick loses much of its power.

The Arms

Go into a back float. Bring both arms to the sides of your body. Keep your chin up and your eyes looking directly overhead.

Begin the stroke by raising your right arm out of the water, palm facing the water, fingers together and wrists relaxed. Keeping your arm straight, swing it in an arc away from the body, so that at the point of entry into the water the palm is about twelve to fourteen inches to the right rear of the head. The hand turns sideways and the little finger enters the water first.

Note that the arm does not go straight up in the air, although many amateur swimmers think it does; actually, that's harder work and less efficient. The arm should move in an arc away from the body, reaching at most a point about two feet above the water.

Now the arm enters the water. Your shoulder dips slightly to help press the arm under the water until the hand is some eight to twelve inches below the surface.

Here's a new term: the *catch*. The catch is the point at which the arm stops its downward movement through the water and starts its power pull through the water to the side of the body. After the catch, the hand forms a straight line with the forearm so as to get the most power from the pull.

The actual pull is a sweeping movement through the water, elbow slightly bent, until the hand reaches the leg. The main power comes from the last twelve inches of the pull. Give an extra whiplike pull to bring your palm to your thigh. Try the stroke several times to get the feel of it. You can move a good way even without kicking.

Co-ordinating the Arms

In the backstroke, one arm enters the water just before the other arm leaves the water to begin the recovery. The timing of arms and legs together is just the same as in the crawl. The stroke follows a six-beat cycle. In other words, here again each arm stroke takes six kicks. *One,* the *right* arm makes the catch (that is, is under water and starts the power pull). *Two, three,* the arm drives to the leg. *Four,* the *left* arm makes its catch; *five* and *six,* the left arm completes its power pull. On *four, five* and *six,* the right arm is making its recovery and re-entering the water and is ready to make its catch again on *one* as the left arm finishes its stroke.

It's probably easiest at first to count one-two-three for each arm and let the recovery take care of itself. But once you have mastered the co-ordination, use the full six counts. To practice the backstroke, go into a back float, set up a steady,

rhythmical kicking, then begin the strokes. Be sure to give the same power to each arm and not favor one over the other.

Breathe freely through the mouth. To help keep all your actions smooth and rhythmical, inhale on the entry of either arm and exhale during the power pull.

Practice until the arms work smoothly together. When you've got it you can tip the chin slightly downward so that your eyes are looking in the opposite direction to the way you're going. Practice until you can backstroke fifty yards.

Some points to remember: Keep your kicking steady. The great mistake beginners make is to kick in erratic bursts which are harder work, and less efficient, than a strong, steady beat.

Lift your arms from the water not vertically but in a horizontal arc. Keep them straight on the recovery.

As your arm enters the water, it's "ridden down" to a depth of about eight inches with a kind of push from the shoulder. The hands should never be more than eight to twelve inches below the surface of the water.

Finish each stroke with a whiplike pull that will give you more power. Here the elbow is slightly bent.

The backstroke is a stroke that many experienced swimmers do incorrectly without realizing it. Instructors will do well to study the text and the drawings with special care before demonstrating the backstroke for the youngsters. The arm stroke and the recovery are particularly important here.

Lesson 18

The Breast Stroke

THE BREAST STROKE probably requires less effort than any other form of swimming. The arm and leg movements are easy and the body is in its most natural floating position. It's the most valuable stroke in heavy seas or open water because it enables you to stay afloat longer than any other form of swimming. It's frequently employed in lifesaving because you can keep an eye on the person in trouble as you approach. In surf swimming, it will enable you to watch the breakers or waves.

The Legs—The Frog Kick

We'll switch the usual order and learn the kick first, because in the breast stroke most of your momentum is supplied by your legs.

The kick is similar to the frog kick you learned in the lesson on the elementary backstroke. To practice it now, take a position in waist-deep water, where you can hold on to the pool railing or the dock or some solid object in the water.

Extend your legs straight back, about six inches below the surface of the water. Now draw your legs into a diamond or wedge shape by bending your knees outward, *not* downward, while keeping your feet as close together as possible and relaxed. Don't bend your hips or waist. Next, turn your ankles outward and spread your legs in as big a V as you can make. After the legs push outward to the V position, the insteps arch.

Keeping your legs straight, bring them swiftly together in a whiplike motion. Only your toes touch at the end of the kick. Glide for a count of three.

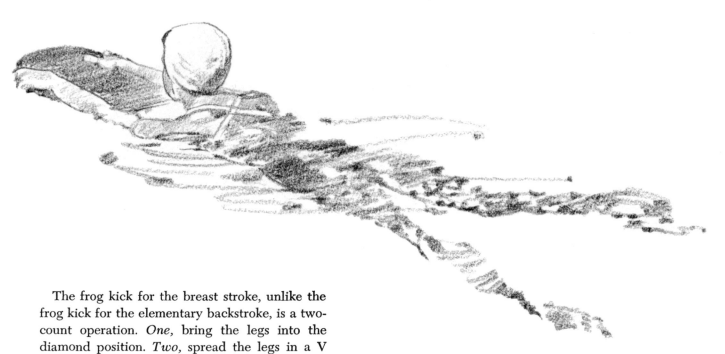

The frog kick for the breast stroke, unlike the frog kick for the elementary backstroke, is a two-count operation. *One,* bring the legs into the diamond position. *Two,* spread the legs in a V and close them in one continuous motion. Don't pause after the V is formed.

The power from the frog kick comes, first, from your instep as your legs push out to form the V and, second, from your instep again as your legs sweep together in the whiplike motion. In both cases, your insteps are acting much like the blades of oars.

Remember, the leg action from diamond to V and sweeping together again is continuous. The kick becomes useless if the legs are jerked outward and then pause.

The Kickboard

The frog kick provides a dandy chance to mention the kickboard again. To repeat what I said about it in Part One, the kickboard is a piece of light wood about two feet long, eighteen inches wide and one inch thick. You hold on to it with your hands, and it gives you enough extra buoyancy to concentrate on your kicking. You can buy one at a sporting-goods store for around $3.95 or you can make one for yourself from pine or balsam wood.

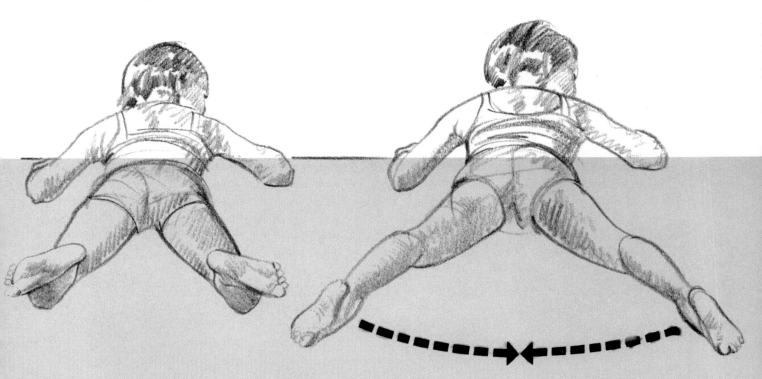

Competitive swimmers use the kickboard all the time to develop their leg muscles. For you, a learner, it's an invaluable device for perfecting your kick technique. Hold on to it; later on it will be fun to play around with in the water.

When you can propel yourself through the water, using the frog kick and holding the kickboard at arm's length, you're ready for the next part of this lesson, which concerns:

The Arms

Stand in waist-deep water with your feet firmly on the bottom. Bend forward until your chest is in the water. Extend your arms in front of you, about three or four inches below the surface of the water. Turn your arms and palms outward so that the backs of your hands face each other. For now, keep your head out of water. For the power part of the stroke, pull your arms away from each other, back through the water until they form a straight line with the shoulders. Your arms should stay about three to four inches below the water.

For the recovery: Turn your arms inward, palms facing each other. Bend your elbows and bring them in close to the body. Bring your hands and forearms under the chin and chest. Now, palms turned downward, straighten the elbows again and extend your arms ahead of you, in position to begin another stroke. Before beginning another stroke, however, you'll glide for a count of three.

Practice until it goes smoothly: stroke, recovery, glide.

Co-ordinating the Arms and Legs

Go into a prone float with your face in the water and your arms extended before you about three inches below the surface. Take a stroke, pulling your arms through the water until they form a straight line with your shoulders.

Now bend your legs into the diamond position and at the same time bend your elbows to bring your hands and forearms under your chin and chest. As you extend your arms before you, spread your legs into a V and quickly close them to give you your thrust. Glide for a count of three. Then begin the cycle again.

74

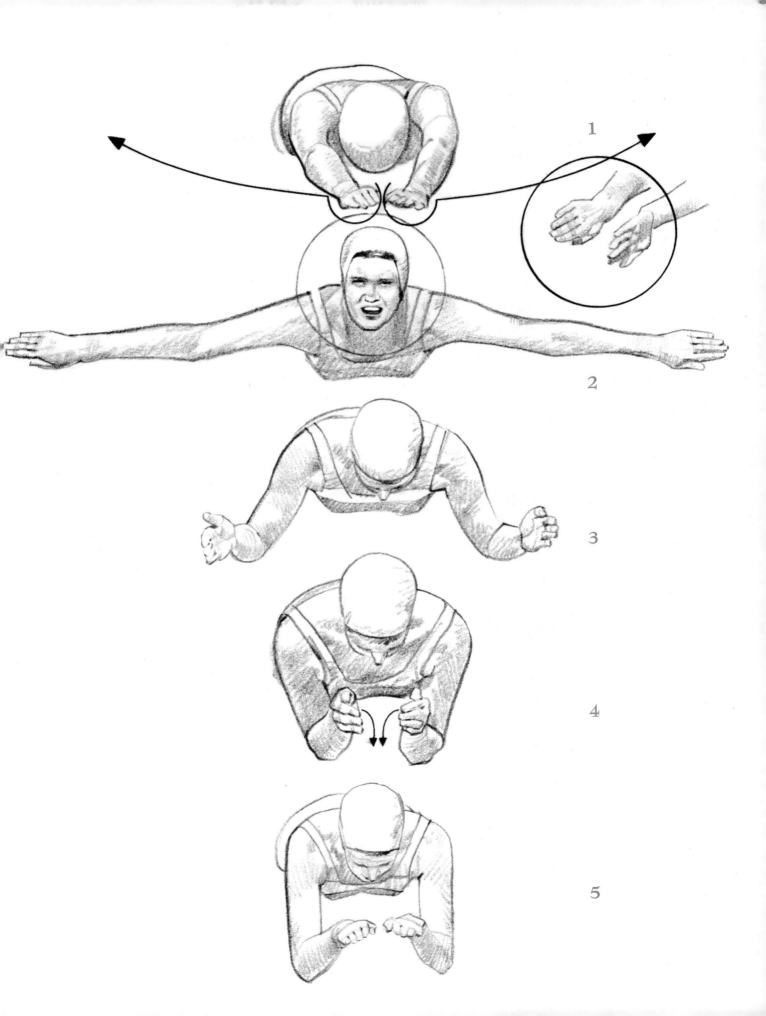

1

2

3

4

5

Remember, the sequence goes like this:

1. ARMS ONLY: Steady pull, no sudden tug.
2. ARMS: Bring elbows to sides, hands and arms under chin.
   LEGS: Feet together, knees outward to form diamond.
3. ARMS: Extend forward.
   LEGS: Thrust apart to form V, then close in one whiplike motion.
4. GLIDE for count of three.

Breathing

You can do the breast stroke with the head above water at all times, and many swimmers do. But after a while the strain on the neck muscles begins to tell, and you defeat the real value of the stroke, which is its effortlessness.

Here is how the head-in-the-water breathing works with the breast stroke:

Again, stand in waist-deep water with your feet firmly planted on the bottom. Bend over until your chest and face are in the water and your arms straight out before you, palms outward. As you start the pull with the arms, lift your face (not your body) from the water and INHALE. When you finish the pull, arms straight out from your shoulders, drop your face into the water and start exhaling, as your elbows bend and your arms and elbows are brought under the chest and chin. Continuing to exhale, glide for the count of three. As you begin a new stroke, lift your head from the water and INHALE.

Practice, standing in waist-deep water, until breathing and the arm motion go smoothly together.

Some of these descriptions may sound formidable. Don't be discouraged. Once you've mastered the crawl, the other strokes will come very easily, almost naturally. The function of the book at this point is to help you make sure you're doing the strokes correctly, in the easiest, most efficient way.

Young learners should practice the stroke with normal breathing until they really have it down cold, before they add the water-breathing technique.

Notice in the drawing below that during the recovery the knees should go outward, not in toward the chest. The leg motion is relaxed.

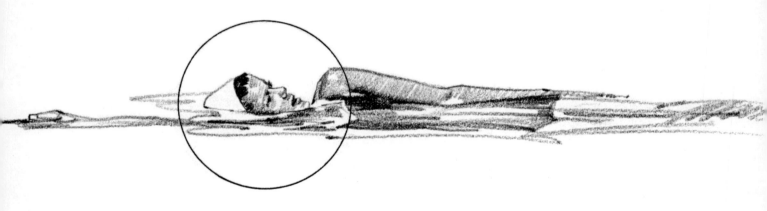

The Side Stroke

IF YOU EVER SAW a rescue in the water, almost certainly you saw the rescuer doing the side stroke. For several reasons, the side stroke is invaluable in safety swimming. The side position enables the swimmer to carry the victim or the rescue equipment. Because he's on his side at all times, the swimmer can breathe naturally, in and out through the mouth. The stroke employs a longer glide than any other stroke and is, there-fore, most restful for the swimmer who may be carrying an added burden. Finally, the swimmer can observe his surroundings or, in endurance swimming, follow a given course.

The stroke, as described below, may sound complicated. Actually, although it differs considerably from the other strokes, it isn't complicated and you'll do well to practice and master it.

The Side Float

As the name suggests, in the side stroke you're literally lying on your side in the water. Here is how to learn the proper body position:

Stand in chest-deep water with your *left* side toward the dock or the side of the pool. Hold on to the dock or pool with your *left* hand. Bend the knees slightly, lowering your body into the water to shoulder level. Extend your *right* arm (which in this case we call the leading arm) *straight* out from the shoulder, about two or three inches below the surface of the water. Lower the *right* side of your face into the water, so that your ear and part of your cheek but *not your mouth* are submerged. Your face should look over your left

shoulder, but the back of your head should remain on the water. It's just like lying on your side in bed, with your arm toward the headboard. Push GENTLY away from the dock or wall and SLOWLY bring the left arm to your side, keeping the arm straight. Shove GENTLY off the bottom with your feet. Bring your legs and feet together, with the ankles arched and the toes pointed, just below the surface. Keep your head in the same position mentioned above or your feet will go to the bottom. Keep your body stretched from your toes to the finger tips of your right hand. Hold the float as long as you can, then repeat it several times so that you can go into it easily.

The secret of getting into the float easily is to shove off the bottom *gently*.

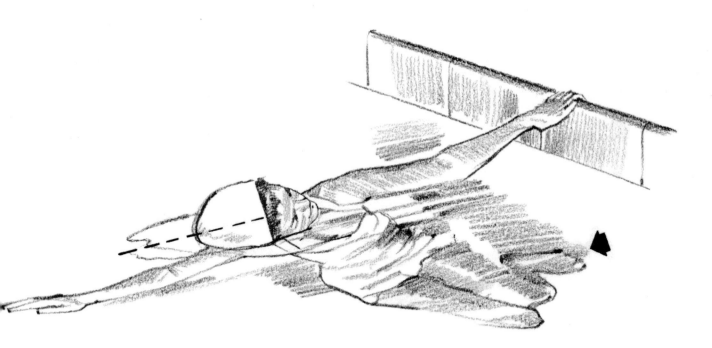

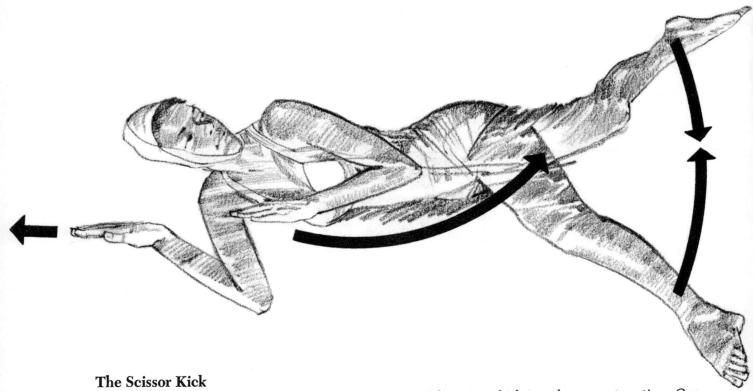

The Scissor Kick

To get the feel of this kick, it's best to try it on dry land first. The name is apt. The legs open to a V and then—snip!—close. Lie on your *right* side on the dock or the edge of the pool, with your legs extending over the edge. Keep your legs together and outstretched. Bend the upper (or left) leg and bring your knee forward until it's level with your hip. Keep the lower part of the leg straight. (It's as if you were going to take a big step upward.) Keep the foot relaxed. At the same time, bend your under leg (the *right* leg) backward from the knee until the foot is opposite the knee. Move the right leg slightly back.

It's from this position that the legs spread to make the V. Straighten the legs in the widest V possible. The lower part of the *left* leg goes forward until the leg is straight. Push the upper part of the *right* leg backward and down from the hip until it's straight.

Instantly, when the legs are in the widest V you can make, snap the legs together again. Keep the toes pointed and the ankles arched. Like the blades of a pair of scissors, the legs stop when they come together at the end of the "snip." Don't allow them to pass each other at the end of the kick.

The scissor kick is a three-count motion: *One,* slowly and relaxed, the legs bend—top leg forward, lower leg back. *Two,* again slowly and relaxed, straighten and spread the legs in a wide V. *Three,* snap the legs together, arch your insteps and extend your toes. The legs are spread and whipped together in one smooth motion. Don't stop at the end of the *two* count. Be careful, too, as you go from the bent-leg position to the V. If the legs are stiffened and jerked into position, you may injure leg or groin muscles.

Try the kick motion on the dock a few times, until you're sure of it. Now, into the water.

As before, go into a side float. The right arm is outstretched and just under the water; the left arm rests on the body. The right ear and cheek are under the water and you look over your left shoulder. Once in the float position, do the kick. Bend the legs, extend them in a V and whip them together. At the end of the whip, hold them motionless and glide through the water. You should glide several feet. As you begin to slow down, kick again. You should have no trouble negotiating the width of the pool or a considerable stretch of the lake, just by scissor-kicking. Remember to keep the back of your head on the water.

80

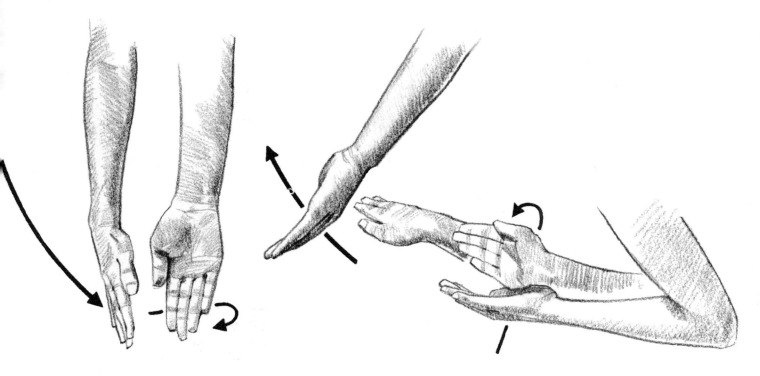

The Arm Stroke

Let's take the left arm first. Try it first standing on dry land. Remember that in the side float the basic position of your left arm is resting along your body. To practice, stand with your left arm resting at your side. Now bring your left hand (palm down) across your chest until the thumb touches your right shoulder. Keep your elbow and forearm close to the body. This is the recovery—the part of the stroke that gets your arm in position for the power stroke. The power stroke is just like brushing a fly off your chest. As the hand presses down and pushes back, the arm straightens across the body until the arm is in its original position alongside the body.

It's a two-step operation: (1) Raise the hand to the right shoulder; (2) press the hand and forearm down across the body.

In the water, let's combine the left-arm stroke with the scissor kick. Go into a side float, the right arm outstretched and just below the surface. Kick and arm go together in three counts:

One: Bring the left hand across the chest to the right shoulder. At the same time, bend the knees to get the legs into position as you learned in count one of the kick.

Two: Keep the hand in place at the shoulder as you straighten the legs into the wide V.

Three: As you whip the legs together in the scissor, press your hand down across the body as if you were shoving the water away.

As you see, your left arm and your legs deliver their power together. For the moment, don't worry about the right arm. Practice the left arm and the kick until they go smoothly together. Make sure your left arm and hand stay close to the body.

Now the right arm. It's called the *lead arm* because it extends out from the shoulder, leading the body. It acts as a rudder, helps to maintain balance, keeps the swimmer from bobbing up and down in the water and supplies propulsion. To veer to the right, the swimmer simply aims the lead arm to the right; to swing left, he points the lead arm leftward.

To practice the lead-arm stroke, stand in shoulder-deep water. Bend from the waist and lean as far as possible to the right. Hold the right arm straight out from the shoulder to the side, palm down. Keeping the arm straight, press down gently and steadily through the water until the fingers point to the bottom. Now the arm is directly beneath the shoulder and underneath the body. Without pausing, keep the upper part of

81

the arm close to the body and turn the hand palm upward. Bring the hand and lower arm slowly upward until the hand is in line with the shoulder, then turn palm downward and extend the hand and arm straight out from the shoulder parallel to the surface of the water. The arm is now back in its starting position. The recovery motion with the lower arm must be done gently or the action will pull you down into the water.

The lead- or right-arm motion is in three counts: *One,* press the arm gently and steadily down through the water until your fingers point to the bottom. *Two,* keeping the elbow and upper arm close to the body, rotate your wrist, turn your palm upward and gently raise your hand up to your shoulder. *Three,* turn your palm down and extend your arm out to its original position. Study the drawing, then practice the stroke, standing a few times.

Co-ordinating the Arms and Legs

Here's how it all goes together. Take a side-float position, right arm outstretched.

One: Press the right arm down through the water until the fingers point to the bottom.

Two: Bring the left hand to the right shoulder and the right hand opposite the right shoulder. At the same time, bend the knees to get the legs into position.

Three: Hold the arms in position and spread the legs in a wide V.

Four: Whip the legs together and simultaneously press the left hand down and push it back across the body, as if shoving water away, and back to your side. As you do, turn the palm down

and extend the right arm to its original supporting position.

Glide a while. During the glide, your left arm is at your side, your right arm outstretched, your legs together with toes pointed and ankles arched.

As you see, the right arm delivers its power first. Then the two arms and the legs go into the recovery. The left arm and the legs deliver their power and, as they do, the right arm completes its recovery.

At first the whole stroke may seem awkward. Practice until you can see how easy and graceful it is. Remember to glide at the end of each stroke. Make sure your body is resting on its side. There should be no bobbing up and down.

The side stroke can be done floating on either side. I've described the right side stroke only to avoid confusion. Once you've mastered the stroke on the right side, try it floating on the left side, letting the left arm become the lead arm, and so on.

On either side, the glide should cover two to four yards. Breathe whenever you want to, but, as in all other strokes, never hold the breath. Inhale and exhale smoothly and regularly. And remember that the correct position of your head determines the proper floating position.

Once children master this stroke, it all seems simple, but getting there is a problem. Demonstrations by Dad are all-important. And he should take it step by step, including the dry runs on the dock, then let the youngsters copy him. They'll learn it easiest by feeling the motions rather than by trying to understand them.

Treading Water

Most earlier swimming books have had little to say about treading water. I think this is a mistake. The ability to stay upright, head above the surface, in water that's over your head is one of the most important skills of watermanship. People who can tread water, as well as float easily, are far more at home—and far safer—than those who can only swim.

The ability to tread water has many applications. It's valuable in the case of a water accident which necessitates your removing your clothes in the water. The tread must be used in changing water positions and in surface diving (which we'll come to later). Like the side stroke, the tread enables you to carry objects across the water without submerging them.

Treading water is not a haphazard movement of arms and legs, but a specific swimming technique, different from the others only in that you're vertical rather than horizontal in the water. Here we'll take up several ways to tread water correctly.

The Sitting Float

As an introduction, and to gain confidence while you're upright in the water, try the sitting float.

Wade out to chin-deep water. Get firmly balanced, then fold your arms across your chest and tuck your hands under your armpits. Tilt your head back on the water and SLOWLY lift your feet from the bottom by raising your knees toward your chest, as if you were in a sitting position. Don't lean backward; remember, this is a sitting float. Do this carefully so that you don't throw your body to one side. Hold your breath as you raise your legs. Once you're in the float you can breathe naturally.

If you start to lose your balance, slowly lower your feet to the bottom again. Remember to keep the head back and the chin up. Try the float several times.

One Way to Tread

Again, stand in chin-deep water. Extend your arms before you, together and about six or eight inches below the surface. Turn the palms outward so that the backs of your hands are together. Sweep your arms apart as far as they'll go comfortably, keeping on the same level, as if you were brushing the water away. Without stopping, turn the palms forward and sweep your arms almost together again, bending the elbows slightly on this return sweep. Still without stopping, turn the palms outward again and sweep outward. The motion is continuous, as if you were first brushing the water away and then gathering it in. The arms should stay ten to twelve inches below the surface all the time, because if you break water you'll start to sink. You'll start to sink also if your arms are too low in the water. The best feeling of balance for you will determine whether your arms should be ten inches or twelve inches below the surface.

84

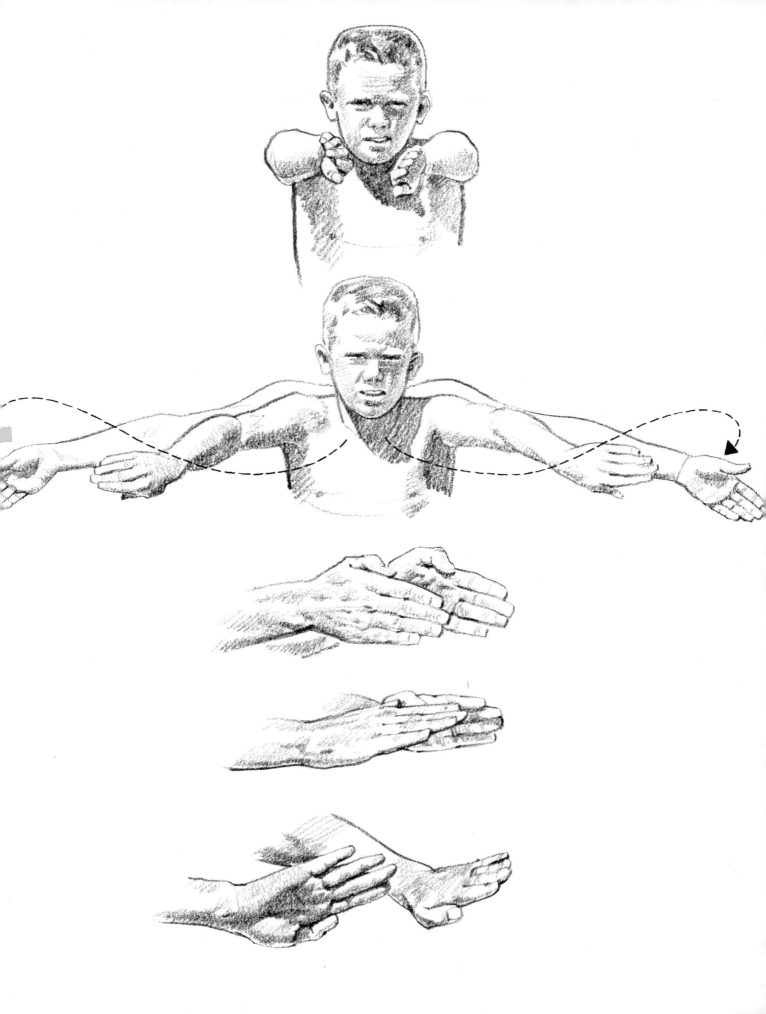

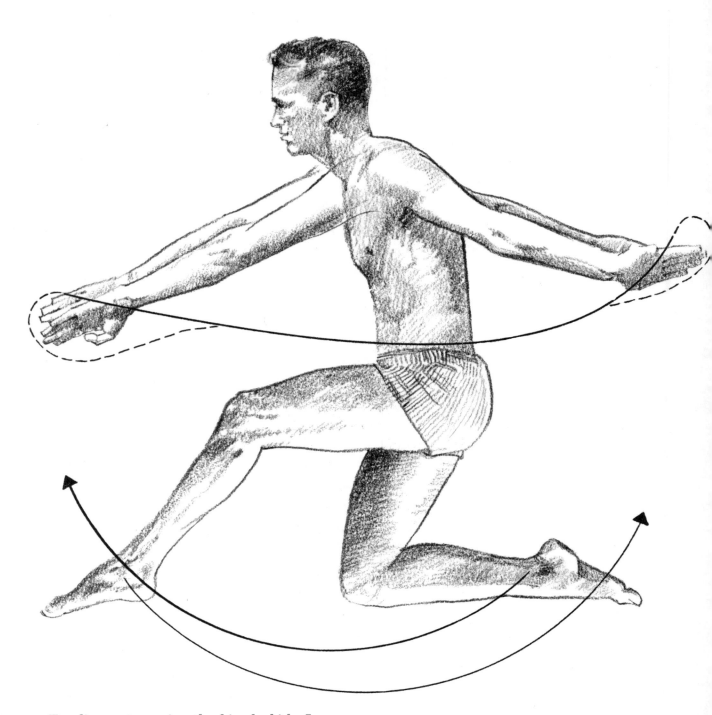

Treading water, using the bicycle kick. Lean
slightly forward, not backward. Swing your arms
as far back as you comfortably can.

86

Continue the sweeping movement of the arms. As you do, tilt the head back, chin up, and lift the knees until you're in a sitting float. Stay in this position, arms moving, for a minute or two. Then drop the legs and rest. Repeat the action until it goes smoothly.

Now start the arm motion, tilt the head back, chin up again. This time, instead of raising the knees in a sitting position, move the legs just as if you were riding a bicycle. The bicycle kick should not be too fast—about four to six kicks to one complete arm stroke, out and back. The bicycle kick is the easiest for a beginner, but there are two others.

The scissor kick learned with the side stroke is used in slightly different form. It's the same kick, but now you're vertical in the water. The right leg bends forward and upward and the left leg bends back to form a V, and then they whip together. Then the left leg bends forward and the right leg bends back and they whip together again. When the left leg is forward, the arms are forward; when the right leg is forward, the arms are back. There are, as you see, just two kick strokes to the complete arm stroke.

The egg beater kick is so called because the legs take turns making a more or less circular movement. Your legs are wider apart for the egg-beater kick. Bend your knee and raise your leg until your thigh is parallel to the surface of the water. Your lower leg is bent under so that the calf almost touches the thigh. Extend, or push, your leg out to the side, straightening the knee. Sweep the leg forward to the center, where the knee bends and the thigh is lifted as before. The action is continuous, and the legs alternate. When the right leg is extended, the left is drawn up, and so on. Try it in the water; the water will help you feel how the kick should go.

I prefer the scissor kick. It's more easily executed and gives better support. I have actually used this kick as a solid support and have been able to shake the water out of a canoe in less than ten seconds in deep water.

Variation on the Arm Stroke

The broad, sweeping movements of the arms in treading water may get tiring after a while. Back in Lesson 7 we practiced *sculling* with the arms. Sculling will now help vary the arm motion in treading water and make it less tiring. It's also added when you're out of co-ordination. Practice it in chin-deep water first.

Sweep the arms outward, palms outward. Then sweep them back together, palms together. This time add two sculling movements. Turn the palms outward and move the arms about two feet apart. Turn the hands inward again and bring them within six inches of each other. Out again about two feet, back together and then a full outward sweep. In other words, make a big outward sweep, then a couple of little sweeps, then another full sweep, and repeat. Be sure to sweep the arms as far back as possible in long arcs. Short sweeps are not necessary unless you've lost co-ordination of your arms and legs and need to move fast to recover.

In treading water, breathe in and out through the mouth at all times, and never hold your breath.

When you can tread water well, go on to the next chapter. To prove that you're the master of treading water, try doing any one of the leg kicks, with both hands held motionless above the water. You should be able to do this for short periods at least. Remember that being able to tread water may one day help you to save another swimmer's life—or your own.

Treading water is part of the requirement for Scout merit badges. On all scores it's a part of swimming that all children should know. The bicycle kick will likely be easiest for young folks. But it's best to have them try all the varieties of treading water until they discover the one they like and can do best. They should then practice it until they can tread for five minutes or more.

Lesson 21

Changing Positions in the Water

I n any long-distance swim in deep water, it's imperative that the swimmer be able to fight fatigue by changing strokes, by going into a motionless float or by treading water. A swimmer who cannot change positions in deep water is in serious trouble. Treading water, beyond its value as a way for the swimmer to rest his muscles and catch his breath, is the best shift position for changing from floating to swimming and back again.

(The old-pro swimmer, as much at home in the water as a trout, may not need the shift position as he alternately floats and swims. But if you're a beginner it's a good point never to overestimate your ability and your strength as a swimmer. You may find you're wrong—the hard way.)

From Tread to Back Float

Tread water as you learned in the last lesson. Gradually change the sweeping movements of the arms to a simple sculling motion at one side of the body. (Sculling is the short in-and-out movement of the hands, alternately gathering water and shoving it away.) Tilt your head back on the water and stop your leg motion. Still sculling, lift your chest and lean back until your feet rise and you're in the back-float position. Then extend your arms out on the water in line with your shoulders, or slightly back. Remember to keep your head back.

From Back Float to Tread

From the back-float position, drop your hips to a sitting position. Pull the head forward and scoop water with the hands down and forward, as explained in Lesson 6 on the back float, and start sculling near your hips. Your legs are tucked under your body. Gradually move the arms to the front, start the broad, sweeping strokes and the bicycle or one of the other kicks.

From Tread to Crawl

Change the sweeping strokes to simple sculling in front of the chest. Lean forward from the waist and slowly push the legs backward to kicking position. When they're in position, start kicking and then begin the arm stroke.

From Crawl to Tread

Stop kicking, lift your head from the water and start sculling. Tuck your knees under your body and start to tread.

From Tread to Breast Stroke and Back

This is the easiest change of all. Simply switch from the sweeping strokes to the breast stroke, lean forward, extend your legs back and begin the frog kick. To go back to treading water, start sculling with the arms, stop kicking long enough for the legs to drop, then start the bicycle kick.

Practice all these changes first in chin-deep water, so that you can touch bottom if you find yourself in trouble.

For children no less than for adults, the important thing here is water safety. Knowing how to change positions in the water spells complete assurance and control by the swimmer. When the swimmer must, accidentally or on purpose, be in the water a long time or cover great distances, changing strokes and positions becomes all-important. These are points the teacher should stress. The swimmer should be made proud of his increasing mastery of the water—and aware of its values.

Lesson 22

Surface Dives

Exploring under water and finding and retrieving sunken objects are among the great—and frequently useful—pleasures of swimming. They begin, most often, with a surface dive, which is simply a technique for heading under water from a swimming position. Here are three variations on the surface dive: the jackknife, the tuck and the fast dive. (If you're interested in ocean swimming, pay special attention to these. As we'll see in Lesson 24, they're useful for getting out of the way of a breaker.)

The jackknife. You can begin the jackknife from either the breast stroke, the side stroke or the crawl stroke. When you reach the spot at

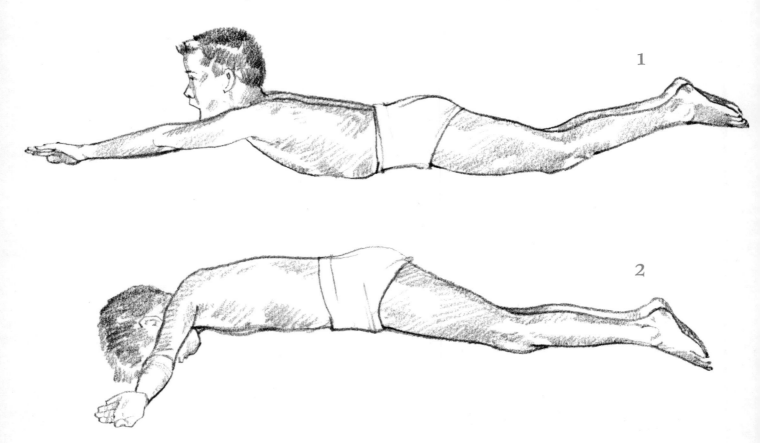

1

2

3

which you wish to dive, halt momentarily. Extend both arms forward in front of your chest, lift your head slightly and take a deep breath as you do in the breast stroke. Pull back hard with both arms, as in treading water, with the arms six to ten inches below the surface. At the same time, bend at the waist in a jackknife and drop your head by tucking your chin in against your chest. Thrust your hips upward. When the upper part of your body is about vertical and the top of your head points at the bottom, move your chin away from your chest so that your gaze is toward the bottom. Stretch your legs upward without bending your knees, making the legs form a straight

4

5

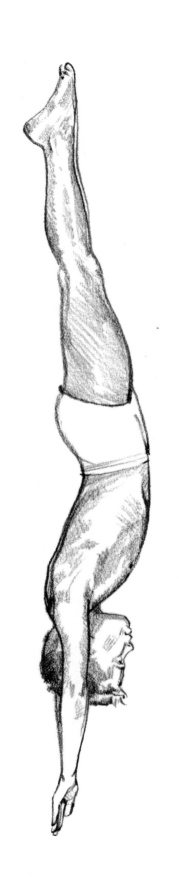

6

line with your body as they slice into the water. To help thrust your legs into the air, push your hips forward like a stripteaser's "bump." Extend your arms forward by turning the palms forward and pressing forward, completing the straight line formed by your trunk and legs. The arms pull back and press forward in a continuous circular movement. Your arms are now in position for swimming. Be sure to keep your legs stiff and your toes pointed and together, so that you're like an arrow slicing into the water.

The position of your head is all-important in the surface dive. If your head stays tucked in against your chest too long, you'll go into a somersault. If it's held away from your chest too long, you won't submerge.

The Fast Dive. This, the most important of the surface dives, begins from a crawl stroke. It's essential to remember that in beginning the fast dive you don't slow down. The dive flows out of the crawl in one continuous sequence.

Begin a regular stroke with the left arm. Make a fast recovery with the right arm, which enters the water only slightly after the left arm. Both arms are in the water straight forward from the head. Drop your head low in the water. Bend sharply from the waist so that your head points downward. Immediately lift your hips and stretch your legs upward, forming a straight line with the body. Keep your legs straight, your toes pointed and together, your ankles arched. Your momentum, plus the weight of your legs, should drive your body beneath the surface six feet or more.

To gain more depth, turn the hands palms outward and pull your arms powerfully in a wide arc until your palms touch your thighs. You should now be ten to fourteen feet below the surface. This is the underwater breaststroke. Ending one stroke, do the breast stroke kick, then glide. Repeat the stroke, kick again, glide again.

To get back to the surface: If you're at the bottom, simply push off with your feet, keeping your hands tight to your sides or extended above your head and together. If you're in deeper water, raise your head well up in the direction of the surface, do a scissor kick, then do the underwater breast stroke—except that now your arms are pulling downward to your sides, forcing you up through the water.

The Tuck. This surface dive begins from a vertical position in the water, as when you're treading water. Force the head and shoulders above the surface of the water by a vigorous scissor kick combined with a downward push of the hands. Hold the body rigid so that you plunge back into the water like an arrow. To give yourself more downward momentum, swing your arms from your sides outward and slightly backward in a circular motion ending with your palms facing forward (keeping the arms unbent), then forward past the line of the hips and upward toward the surface (with elbows bent). This can be repeated two or three times to get the depth required.

Now, vertical in the water and three or more feet below the surface, do the tuck. Pull your knees to your chest and at the same time drop your chin as low as possible until it rests against your chest. Clasp your arms around your legs and swing your hips toward the surface, rolling forward in the water. Straighten your legs so that they point upward, and raise your head from your chest so that your eyes point downward. Straighten your arms and extend them downward, so that the whole body forms a straight line. From this position you can begin the underwater breast stroke to continue your descent or to level out.

In all surface diving, there are some warnings to bear in mind. Be mindful of underwater obstructions: pilings, boulders on the bottom. Keep your eyes open and, if visibility is poor, your arms before you. Let your arms—not your head and neck—be your bumpers.

Successful surface diving opens up a whole new world of pleasure. It may even lead to flippers, face masks, air tanks and all the paraphernalia of skin diving—but that's another book.

Long before skin diving became an adult passion, the kids were spending half their swimming time under water, retrieving tin cans, exploring rocks and pilings and playing tag. Beyond its practical aspects, underwater swimming opens up a new world of pleasure. Surface diving is the open-sesame, and your youngsters will want to learn it, for the fun of it.

The bent-arm recovery, shown by Ann Curtis Cuneo.

Lesson 23

Championship Techniques
in the Crawl

THE DIFFERENCE between the golfer who goes around in 68 and the golfer who shoots 88 is not really great. They use the same clubs and from a distance their swings may seem to be identical. The real difference between the champion and the talented amateur is the sum of many small points of technique, mastered by the pro but only occasionally conquered by the amateur.

If you'll allow me this long comparison, the same condition is true of championship swimming. Perfection in the American crawl is a combination of rigorous training plus an almost finicky attention to details. In this lesson, I'm going to talk about the stroke as I've taught it to all my champions—Ann Curtis, Marilyn Sahner, Delia Meulenkamp, Marion Pontacq, Barbara Jensen, all those wonderful girls who have held over sixty national and world records. Once you've mastered the elementary crawl as I outlined it in Lessons 11 through 13, I think you'll want to tackle this championship, competitive version of the crawl.

You may remember that in Lesson 11 I introduced you to the question of the straight-arm recovery versus the bent-arm recovery. For the beginning swimmer, I insisted that the straight-arm recovery was the best way to learn because it avoids the formation of awkward arm movements and positions. For speed swimming, whether you use the straight-arm recovery or the bent-arm recovery depends on your physical attributes. If you have long arms and long legs, are tall and of slender build, use the bent-arm recovery described below. If you're thick-chested and have short arms and legs, you may find the straight-arm recovery described in Lesson 11 easier for you.

The Bent-Arm Recovery

In the straight-arm recovery, you'll remember, after your hand has brushed your thigh to complete the power stroke, you raise your arm (bent only slightly) out of the water and swing it over the water in a low, sweeping arc to its original position, pointing straight ahead. Here is how the bent-arm recovery works:

It begins, as always, after your hand brushes the lower part of your thigh to complete the power stroke. Raise your arm completely out of the water by lifting your elbow. Your arm now forms a right angle, with your forearm and hand hanging straight down from the elbow in a relaxed position. Throughout the recovery, your hand—fingers together—stays just above the water, not touching the water.

Keeping your elbow HIGH (study the picture carefully), use your upper arm to push your hand and forearm forward. Your hand remains at a constant level above the water. As you push forward, your arm gradually straightens to its natural length (don't overreach) until the hand is in position to begin its new stroke. The hand's point of entry into the water is almost directly ahead of the eye. Your arm doesn't straighten completely but remains slightly bent as it lies on the water and throughout the power stroke to follow.

REMEMBER: Keep your elbow HIGH throughout the recovery. Keep your hand just off the water;

never let it go as high as your shoulder or elbow. As it moves forward over the water it describes a straight line, as shown in the picture. Don't let your hand and forearm swing out to the side or in too close to the body.

Another note: No two people have identical bone or muscular structure. For that reason, no two people walk exactly alike or swim exactly alike. In terms of the bent-arm recovery, some people may find that they cannot easily lift their elbows higher than their shoulders. If this is true for you, you can—in order to get your hand clear of the water—swing your forearm out to the side. You should swing your arm out *only* far enough to let your hand stay above the water. The object of the bent-arm recovery is to get your hand and arm into position for a new stroke the fastest possible way. Since the shortest distance between two points is a straight line, the more you have to swing your arm off the straight line to the side the slower your recovery will be.

The *only* variation in the bent-arm recovery is this slight swing to the side by the forearm and and hand. The shoulder should never drop, nor should the hand be raised higher than the shoulder.

However the recovery is made, the power stroke through the water remains the same for all swimmers. Before we practice the bent-arm recovery, I'd like to reiterate a few points about the power stroke. These are the small details that make all the difference between good swimming and championship swimming:

1. From the point of entry ahead of the eye, the hand presses straight down through the water and begins the pull back. Near the end of the pull motion, the arm veers outward very slightly to complete the push back to the thigh.

2. The arm remains slightly bent throughout the pull to give more pressure against the water than the straight arm would give.

3. Throughout the stroke the hand keeps the same position relative to the wrist. Fingers are together and the hand is neither cupped downward nor bent backward from the wrist. It's in the same position it would have if the hand and arm were resting on a table top.

4. Don't "reach for the bottom" during the power stroke. Many swimmers assume that this will give them more power, but actually this

movement only pulls the shoulder deeper into the water and impedes your progress.

5. Don't let the arm waver, as in sculling, or turn in under the body. All these motions will make the body roll from side to side in the water and greatly impede your motion.

6. Remember the extra whiplike motion as you complete the push and the stroke. The whiplike motion will give you an added touch of power.

Practicing the Championship Stroke

Even though you're already a swimmer, it makes sense to practice the stroke and the bent-arm recovery, or straight-arm recovery, while bending over in waist-deep water, as you did when you were learning the elementary crawl.

Practice the arms separately first. Bend over in waist-deep water, arms extended before you on the surface of the water. Press, pull and push through the water, remembering insofar as you can the points I've made above.

Raise your elbow, letting the hand and forearm hang down from the elbow. Keeping the elbow HIGH, push the hand and forearm forward to the original position. After a few tries with each arm, check yourself against the pictures. The single most important point is to keep your elbows high. It may help to imagine a string tied to your elbow; puppetlike, lift your elbow high out of the water and then swing it forward to begin the new stroke.

Starting with the arms together, this is the sequence: As the *right* arm starts the push back, the *left* arm starts the press down. As the *right* arm completes the push back, the *left* arm starts the pull. As the *left* arm pulls, the *right* arm is being recovered and brought forward. As the *left* arm is pushing back, the *right* arm starts its press down, and so on. This is the perfect timing. At first some swimmers may have trouble mastering it, but this is the timing as it should be, and the timing you should strive for.

The importance of the fast, bent-arm recovery should now be clear. In the championship crawl both arms are in the power stroke at the same time. One arm should have been "ridden down" and the pull begun before the other arm has completed the push and been drawn out of the water.

After the in-place practice of the strokes, try swimming with your head out of water. Watch your arms work and try to correct any faults you may be making, before you go on to combine the stroke with breathing.

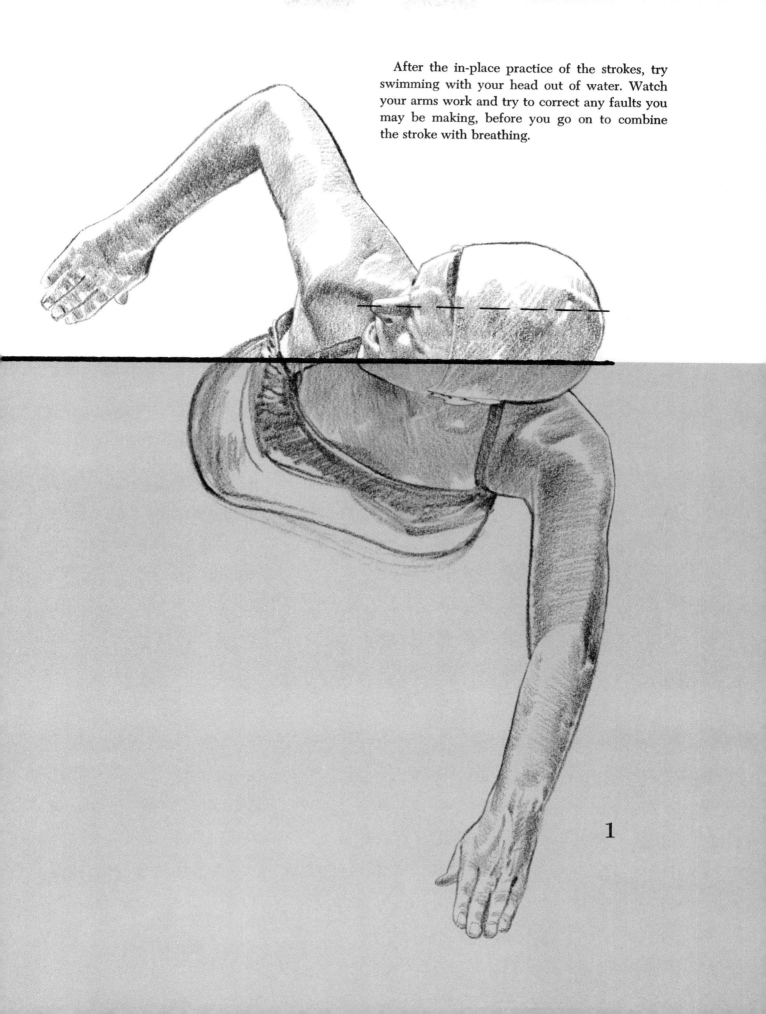

1

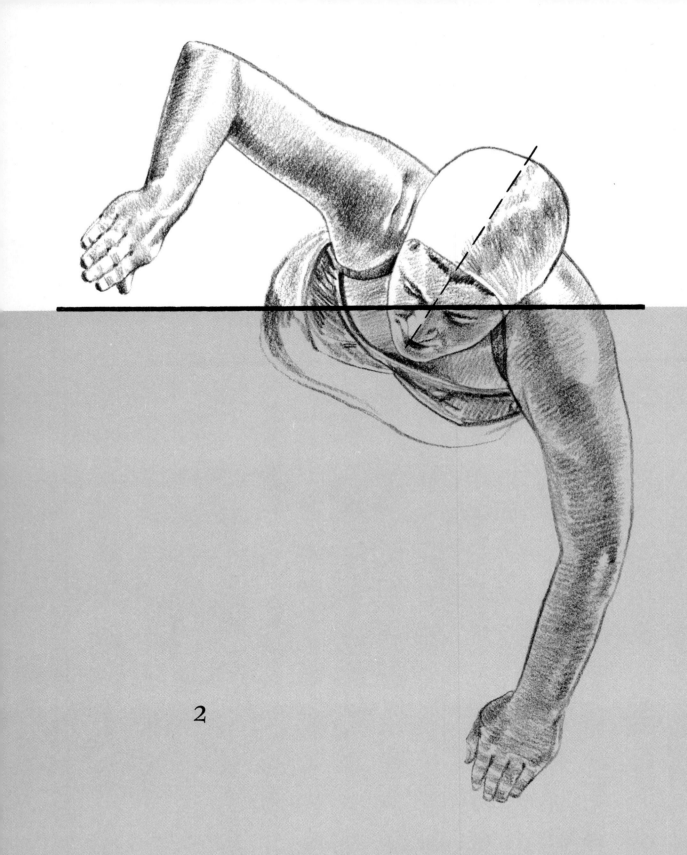

2

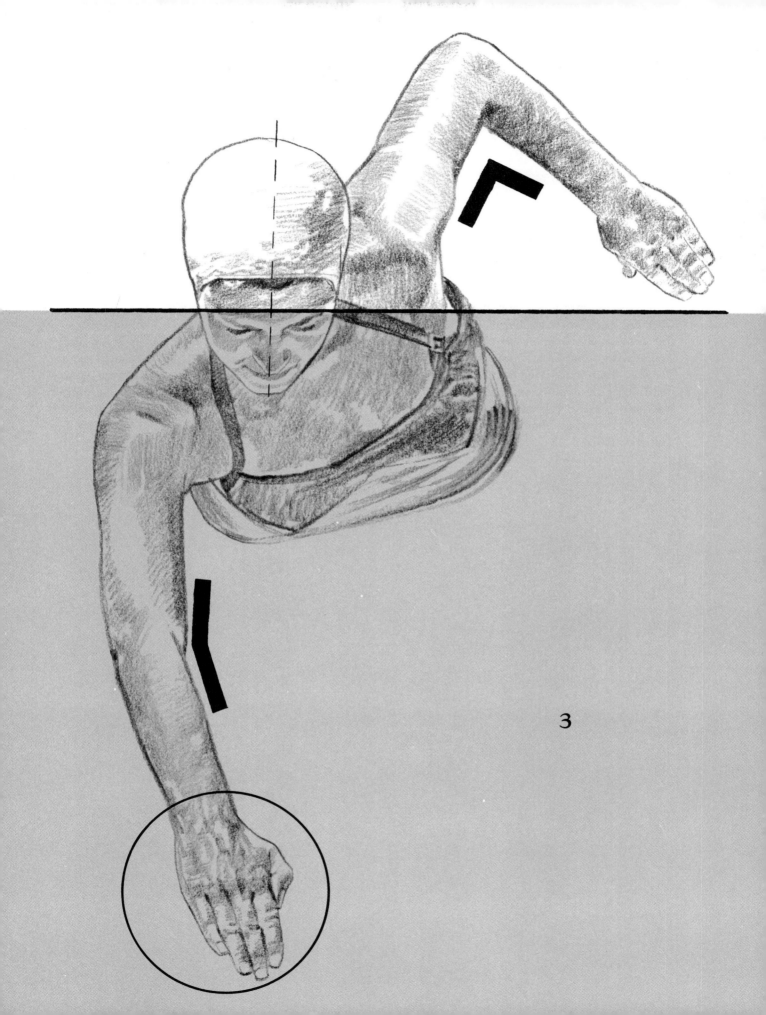

3

Breathing

In the lessons on the elementary crawl, I explained the vital importance of deep breathing. In the championship crawl, your muscular activity is of course much greater. Accordingly, your muscles burn much more oxygen and you're creating more waste carbon dioxide which must be fully expelled from the lungs to prevent fatigue. Improper breathing is the most common fault of even good swimmers. Be *sure* you're exhaling fully and breathing as deeply as is necessary. It will take more practice to master the breathing cycle than any part of championship swimming.

You can breathe on either the right or left side.

In practice and in competition you should alternate, swimming one lap breathing to the right and one lap breathing to the left. This will even the arm-stroke pull. And in races you will not have a blind side and will be able to see your competitors. To review briefly, let me describe the breathing on the right side. Your head is in the water to the brow line and, like that orange on the end of a stick, it does not move up and down but only swivels to one side or the other.

As your right arm starts its push, turn your head to the right, nose and mouth out of water, and as your right arm recovers INHALE. As the arm moves forward, the head instantly re-enters the water. EXHALE through slightly compressed lips as your head turns first to center front and

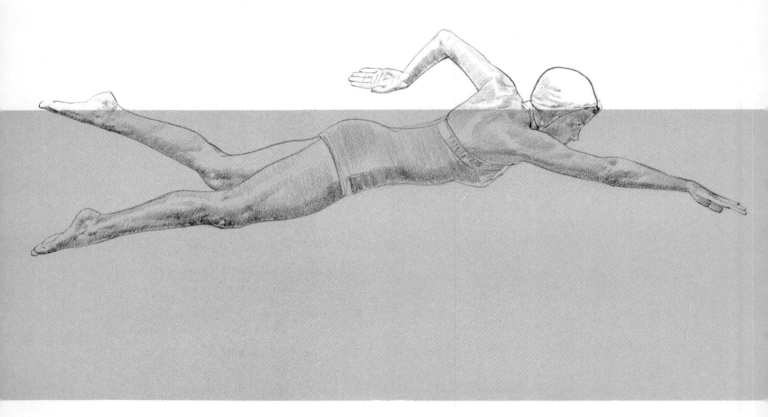

then back to the right.

Let me explain again, as I did in Lesson 2, why it makes sense to exhale through slightly compressed lips. In the first place, you can control the rate of breathing more accurately. This is important because you should never hold your breath, as I've explained before, and it takes practice to time your exhaling so that your lungs are completely emptied at the moment your mouth breaks above water and you're ready to inhale again. Keeping the lips compressed also prevents water from entering your mouth. Finally, you can more completely empty your lungs if you exhale through slightly compressed lips. Try it both ways, kneeling in the water, and see if you don't agree.

The Kick

To develop leg, ankle and thigh muscles that can maintain the pace of sprint swimming requires almost endless practice. Back in Lesson 18, I discussed the kickboard. At this point, a kickboard is a must. Latch on to a kickboard, remember to breathe normally, and kick yourself from one end of the pool to the other. You should kick a thousand yards each time you go swimming—about three time a week for proper conditioning, or every day if possible.

The kick as I teach it is considerably different from the usual flutter kick taught with the crawl, and I'd like to say a little bit about how it works and why I teach it.

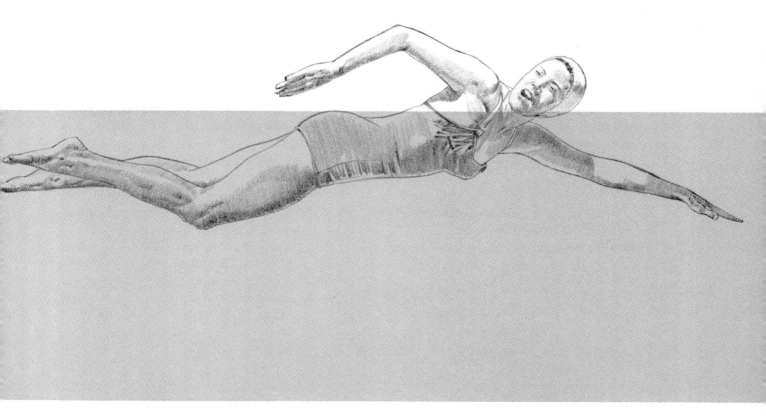

The major difference between the kick as I teach it and the flutter kick is that in my kick the leg is *not* held stiff as a board. The power in the kick starts at the hips and flows down the relaxed legs. The knees are not kept stiff; any effort in the calf muscles to keep the knees stiff quickly produces fatigue. The knees don't bend a lot but move naturally, as the hip muscles and the heavy thigh muscles do the bulk of the leg work. The depth of the kick—that is, the distance the feet move apart—varies with your speed as I'll describe later on. The legs should pass as close to each other as possible without touching and without your forcing them together unnaturally. Occasionally the heels and insteps may leave the water, but at no time should the whole foot leave the water. If it does, it reduces your power by requiring force to break the surface of the water again. On the other hand, if the legs are too low in the water the kick becomes negative.

The kick motion is, then, a whiplike thrash. For my money, it's ideal for long, uninterrupted kick action, and here is why:

The value of the bent-arm recovery, in addition to its greater speed, is that it affords a brief moment of rest for the long muscles of the forearm and upper arm. These muscles are apt to tire most easily. The muscles used in the bent-arm recovery are less apt to tire.

I discovered that there's a similar period of recovery in the legs. It's that time (admittedly very short) when the leg is returning toward the surface of the water. By whipping the kick from the strong hip and thigh muscles, the leg has a brief moment of rest during the recovery. When the calf muscles are used heavily in the kick or in keeping the leg straight, they quickly tire and soon impede the entire leg action. You might try it both ways for a short distance and see if you don't discover the same thing.

At first, the relaxed kick seemed mostly valuable for distance swimming. I later applied it to sprints by narrowing the scope or depth of the kick. It proved to be faster than any other kick, even for sprints. (As a test, I once pitted Olympic champion Ann Curtis against some very competent swimmers. The other swimmers used both arms and legs. Ann, using her legs only, defeated them.)

Arms and legs have to be balanced—equally powerful—for top-notch swimming. Ann Curtis, when she became my pupil, had a powerful kick but comparatively weak arms and was a vastly discouraged swimmer. When she once developed her arms, after continual practice, she was on her way to her subsequent national and Olympic triumphs. And she was equally skilled in the sprint and distance events.

Co-ordination

In Lesson Fourteen, Mastering the American Crawl, you saw how each full arm stroke—from the time the hand enters the water until it is ready to enter the water again—takes six kicks. This is the six-beat crawl. And the same relationship—six kicks to every full arm stroke—is maintained wether you are swimming fast or slow. The rate at which your arms move governs how fast you breathe and how fast you kick. (A few swimmers go to an eight-beat or even a ten-beat crawl: eight or ten kicks to every complete arm stroke. This is a really strenuous pace. The six-beat crawl is standard and I think rightly so.)

At a slow, steady pace, as in distance swimming, the *depth* of your kick is about equal to your stride while you're walking. The faster you swim, the shallower your kick becomes. This works out automatically, as you'll see when you try it. Obviously, the only way your kick can sustain its six-beat relationship to your arms when they're moving at high speed is for your feet to travel a shorter distance. Because his feet thus stay nearer the surface, a sprint swimmer churns up a furious wake.

Two important points to remember: the feet break the surface, but they do not leave the water completely. And no matter how fast you kick, the legs keep loose and relaxed, not locked stiff at the knee. It is still the whiplike thrash.

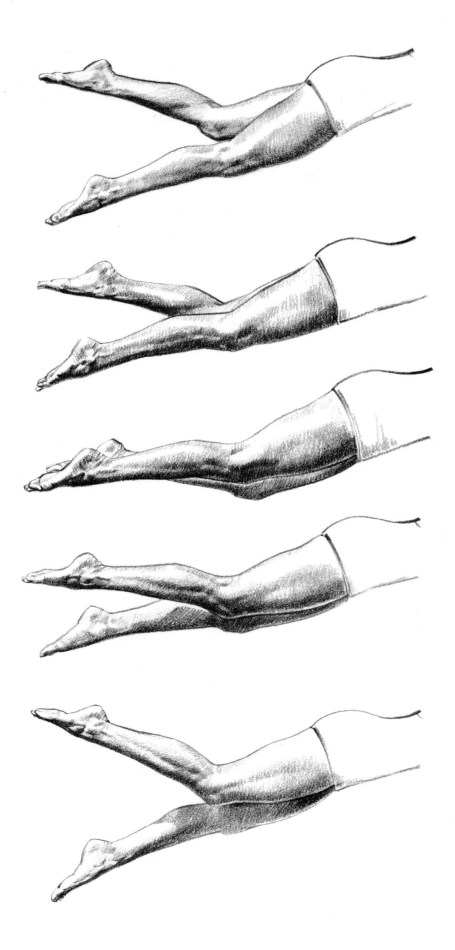

Lesson 24

Swimming in the Surf

SWIMMING IN POOLS or fresh water is fun. But to anyone who has ever tried it, nothing begins to compare with the thrill of swimming in the ocean. The ocean swimmer uses his skill to harness the power and immensity of the surf, maneuvering on top of a huge wave and being carried swiftly and effortlessly to shore, finding in his achievement a sense of freedom and exhilaration virtually unique in the world of sport. He gets a lift in more ways than one, for salt water is heavier than fresh water and gives him added buoyancy.

Surf swimming is not for the beginner or the uncertain swimmer. But for anyone who is at ease and confident in the water, able to float and surface dive, the ocean presents an irresistible attraction.

Before you enter the water, be sure to check tide conditions with the lifeguards on duty. These tide conditions vary from day to day at any beach. In particular you should inquire about the *sweep*. The sweep is a lateral motion of the surface water, caused by the prevailing wind. It can fool you, because the waves may very likely be striking the beach head on and yet the surface water may be sweeping to right or left, parallel to the beach. The danger is that if you're unaware of the sweep it can imperceptibly carry you off course. Finding yourself off course, you can easily exhaust yourself trying to buck the sweep. Find out if there is one, and which way it's moving. Then, when you're in the water and want to return to shore, head for the beach at an angle. The sweep may still carry you off course, but you'll make headway. Don't try to fight it. It becomes a problem only if you're unaware of it or don't know how to handle it.

Remember, too, that every beach has its own unique characteristics—holes, sand bars, channels—and all of them affect the behavior of the tide. This is because water always seeks the lines of least resistance. Let's take a couple of examples.

When the shore line is curved, it may present something called a sea puss or rip tide. This is in effect an outgoing current within the tide. It's a channel of foaming water a few yards wide (never more than twenty yards), deeper and more powerful than the current to each side. It exists because the contours of the beach send more water funneling into the channel. The swimmer caught in the sea puss finds that he can make no headway. Should you find yourself in the sea puss, let it carry you seaward until you have your bearings. Then begin swimming, not toward shore but into the calmer water to either side of the sea puss.

Sand bars exist at almost every beach and present problems of their own. When they're submerged, the water tends to be calmer above them and suddenly stronger to each side. The swimmer finds the going easy while he's right above them, then finds himself in the deeper water and the stronger current.

At any beach, too, there may be old pilings, submerged rocks or other hazards not immediately evident. As with all the beach conditions, these are troublesome only if you're not aware of them.

Heading into the Surf

Walk into the water, knees high, leaning slightly forward, digging your toes into the sand as firmer footing against the undertow.

Now you're in waist-deep water and a breaker is approaching. Your aim is to get beyond it to the calmer seas. (It may also knock you over if you just stand there.) Just as the wave breaks, or a split second beforehand, dive under the base of the wave. Aim low and take a stroke, pulling with the arms as in the breast stroke, to get beyond the breaker so that you can surface and look for

the next breaker. Breakers seem to come in series of three, with the last one usually the largest.*

Breakers in Deep Water

You should now be in the majestically serene and gently swelling seas out beyond the breakers. But if you see another big breaker coming, take a quick, deep breath and, holding your body rigid, duck under the water. To do this, keep your elbows close to your sides and push upward with your hands and forearms. You should submerge a yard or more to escape the force of the breaker. When it has passed, paddle yourself to the surface again.

The surface dive provides another way to avoid a breaker. We've talked about surface diving in Lesson 22. It's a good thing to review and practice before you try the surf.

Picking a Wave

Now you're ready to pick a wave for the ride to shore. Have a look at the drawings. Picking the wrong wave can give you a dunking instead of a ride. What you want is a roller, not a breaker.

In general, a breaker will seem to be steeper and more sharply peaked. Breakers are aptly named. The crest breaks sharply with a distinct crash. When it does, if you're unlucky enough to be on top of it, you can be dumped to the ocean bottom with sudden and dangerous force. A breaker may often be foamier than a roller. A roller, on the other hand, will be broader, more rounded, less sharply peaked. It will travel farther. By spending some time on shore watching the waves, you'll quickly learn to distinguish breakers and rollers. You'll know the breakers by their crashing, noisy collapse and you'll learn to spot them before they break.

If, later on, you pick a breaker by mistake and

---

* For a wonderful description of the technique and the sensations of surf riding, read Eugene Burdick's novel, *The Ninth Wave* (Houghton Mifflin, 1956). Burdick's characters hold that the ninth wave is the big one and that the ninth wave of the ninth series—the eighty-first wave—is the greatest of all.

are dumped, try to roll yourself into a ball and ride it out. Double up your legs, wrap your arms around your knees and tuck your head down.

In picking a wave to ride, realize that the timing involved in getting atop a wave is tricky and takes practice. Waves, of course, vary in size and speed. Pick one that matches your abilities— smaller, slower ones at first.

Riding the Surf

Now you're ready for the real fun, riding a wave. Heading toward shore, look back and choose an approaching wave. As it reaches you, you'll feel yourself simultaneously being lifted and pulled backward. As you start to rise, take several fast strokes and kick hard. Your aim is to match your speed with that of the wave until you're atop it and it carries you. When the wave starts to carry you, keep your head high but scrunch your shoulders together as if you were cold. Keep your legs straight and together. You can keep on kicking or not, as you prefer. Some surf swimmers kick; others don't. You can keep your arms at your sides, with your elbows bent slightly away from the body. Or, you can hold your hands, back to back, between your legs. Either way you're riding the crest of the wave and you go zooming toward shore by courtesy of the ocean's enormous power. It's an incredible experience, one you won't fully appreciate until you've tried it yourself.

When the force of the wave is spent, you should be almost ashore, ready to scramble onto the beach, brag a little—and start all over again.

Some Cautionary Notes

Waves are like streetcars; there's always another one coming. A cardinal lesson of surf swimming is: WATCH OUT FOR THE NEXT ONE. If you're accidentally knocked over by a wave near shore or dumped by a breaker farther out, remember that there's another wave close behind. Don't let yourself be caught off guard.

If you can avoid it, never swim alone. One swimmer can easily be lost sight of in the immensity of the surf, even at a beach with lifeguards.

If you find yourself farther out than you intended to get, keep calm and head back to shore in easy stages. You can float or tread water to rest your arms. Take advantage of the rollers and make them give you a ride. The advice given early in this book to keep calm and take it easy applies in the ocean no less than in a pool. The ocean is bigger and stronger than you are, but you're smarter.

And may you find, as so many have, that surf riding is to swimming what the World Series is to baseball, the greatest challenge and the greatest reward that the sport has to offer.

Lesson 25

Artificial Respiration

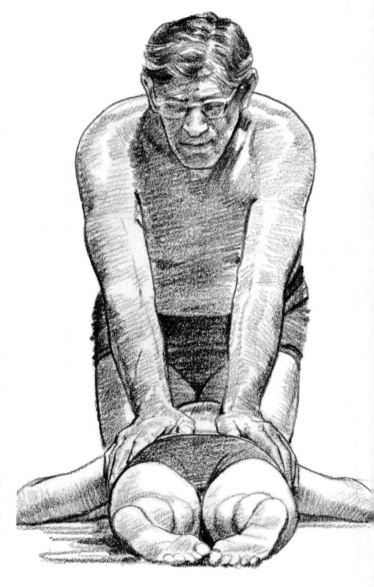

THE INFORMATION in this chapter can help you save a life. I hope you'll never have occasion to use it, but you should know it. Please—for the sake of someone you may not now even know—study the two methods in this chapter carefully.

Artificial respiration should be started as quickly as possible. It should be continued a long time—two hours if need be—until normal breathing returns or until there's no longer any hope at all.

Prone Pressure Method

1. Lay the subject prone, face down. If possible, find a spot of ground where the head can be slightly lower than the rest of the body, to facilitate draining the air passage. Be sure the tongue is flat and that no foreign objects are blocking the throat. The chin should not sag, lest it obstruct the wind passage.

Bend the subject's elbows, place one hand atop the other. Turn his face to one side and lay it on his hands.

2. Kneel facing the subject, with your knees touching his forearms. If you prefer, kneel on one knee only, placing your other foot near his elbow. Imagine a line running across the subject's back from armpit to armpit. Place your hands on the flat of the subject's back, with the heels of your hands just below this imaginary line. Your thumb tips should just touch. Spread your fingers downward and outward.

3. Lean forward, keeping your elbows straight, until your arms are vertical. Let the weight of your upper body exert slow, even pressure on your hands. This forces air out of the lungs.

4. Release the pressure (don't give a final push). Slowly rock backward. As you go, put your hands on the subject's arms just above the elbow.

5. Lift his arms upward and toward you as you rock backward. Apply just enough lift to feel resistance at the subject's shoulders. Don't bend your elbows. Now lower his arms to the ground again. This completes the breathing cycle. Lifting his arms expanded the chest by pulling the chest muscles, arching the back and relieving the weight on the chest.

Repeat the cycle about twelve times per minute at a steady rate. The push and the pull (exhale and inhale) should get about equal time. The important thing is to keep the rhythm smooth and continuous.

Once normal breathing returns, keep the subject flat and warm for some time, until a doctor comes or recovery seems complete.

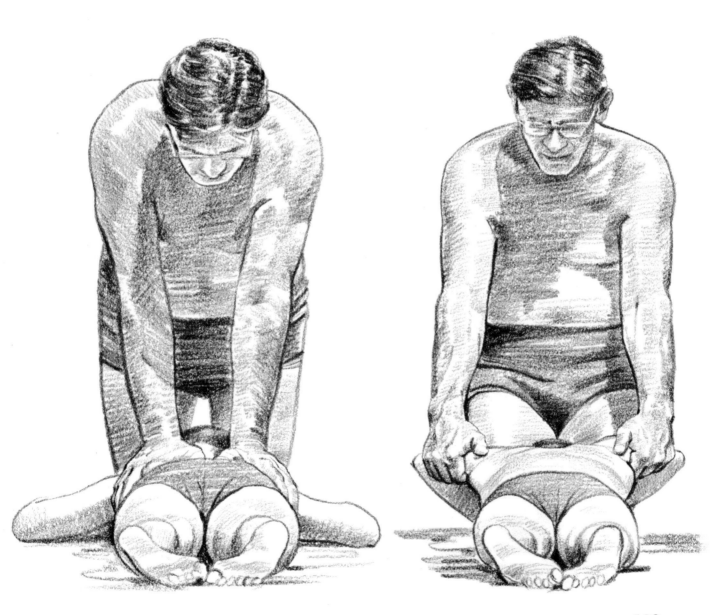

109

An alternate method of artificial respiration is the mouth-to-mouth technique recently adopted for its first aid and water safety training courses by the American National Red Cross. This organization has kindly allowed us to reproduce the method (which follows in its entirety) from the 1959 supplement to their First Aid Textbook.

Mouth-to-Mouth (Mouth-to-Nose) Method of Artificial Respiration

If there is foreign matter visible in the mouth, wipe it out quickly with your fingers or a cloth wrapped around your fingers.

1. Tilt the head back so the chin is pointing upward (Fig. 1). Pull or push the jaw into a jutting-out position (Fig. 2 and Fig. 3).

These maneuvers should relieve obstruction of the airway by moving the base of the tongue away from the back of the throat.

4

5

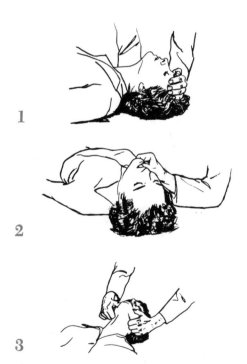

1

2

3

6

2. Open your mouth wide and place it tightly over the victim's mouth. At the same time pinch the victim's nostrils shut (Fig. 4) or close the nostrils with your cheek (Fig. 5). Or close the victim's mouth and place your mouth over the nose (Fig. 6). Blow into the victim's mouth or nose. (Air may be blown through the victim's teeth, even though they may be clenched.)

The first blowing efforts should determine whether or not obstruction exists.

3. Remove your mouth, turn your head to the side, and listen for the return rush of air that indicates air exchange. Repeat the blowing effort.

For an adult, blow vigorously at the rate of about 12 breaths per minute. For a child, take relatively shallow breaths appropriate for the child's size, at the rate of about 20 per minute.

4. If you are not getting air exchange, recheck the head and jaw position (Fig. 1 or Fig. 2 and Fig. 3). If you still do not get air exchange, quickly turn the victim on his side and administer several sharp blows between the shoulder blades in the hope of dislodging foreign matter (Fig. 7).

Again sweep your fingers through the victim's mouth to remove foreign matter.

Those who do not wish to come in contact with the person may hold a cloth over the victim's mouth or nose and breathe through it. The cloth does not greatly affect the exchange of air.

7

Mouth-to-Mouth Technique for Infants and Small Children

If foreign matter is visible in the mouth, clean it out quickly as described previously.

1. Place the child on his back and use the fingers of both hands to lift the lower jaw from beneath and behind, so that it juts out (Fig. 8).

2. Place your mouth over the child's mouth AND nose, making a relatively leakproof seal, and breathe into the child, using shallow puffs of

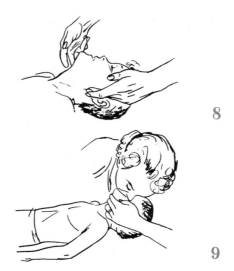

8

9

air (Fig. 9). The breathing rate should be about 20 per minute.

If you meet resistance in your blowing efforts, recheck the position of the jaw. If the air passages are still blocked, the child should be suspended momentarily by the ankles (Fig. 10) or inverted over one arm (Fig. 11) and given two or three sharp pats between the shoulder blades, in the hope of dislodging obstructing matter.

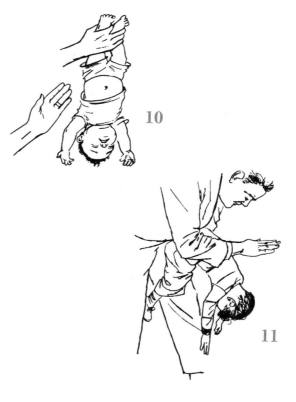

10

11

Conclusion

As THE MAN SAYS, that's all there is, there isn't any more. I hope you've found that the book helped you to swim. If you have got discouraged anywhere along the way, remember that there are very, very few "natural" swimmers. Most of the good swimmers have got that way by patience and hard work.

I hope my little book has been or will be your passport to a long lifetime of safe and pleasurable swimming. I wish you many a long hour of the healthiest, most relaxing, pleasantest sport on earth.

Come on in, the water's fine.